PATERNOSTER
INVESTIGATIONS

BBC
DOCTOR WHO
ROLEPLAYING GAME

CREDITS

WRITING: Walt Ciechanowski and Andrew Peregrine
EDITING: Andrew Kenrick
COVER: Paul Bourne
GRAPHIC DESIGN AND LAYOUT: Paul Bourne
CREATIVE DIRECTOR: Jon Hodgson
PUBLISHER: Dominic McDowall
PROOFREADERS: Peter Gilham and Brian Swift
SPECIAL THANKS: Ross McGlinchey and the BBC team for all their help.

The **Doctor Who Roleplaying Game** uses the Vortex system, designed by David F. Chapman.

Published by Cubicle 7 Entertainment Ltd
Suite D3 Unit 4 Gemini House, Hargreaves Road,
Groundwell Industrial Estate, Swindon, SN25 5AZ, UK.
(UK reg. no.6036414).

Find out more about us and our games at
www.cubicle7.co.uk

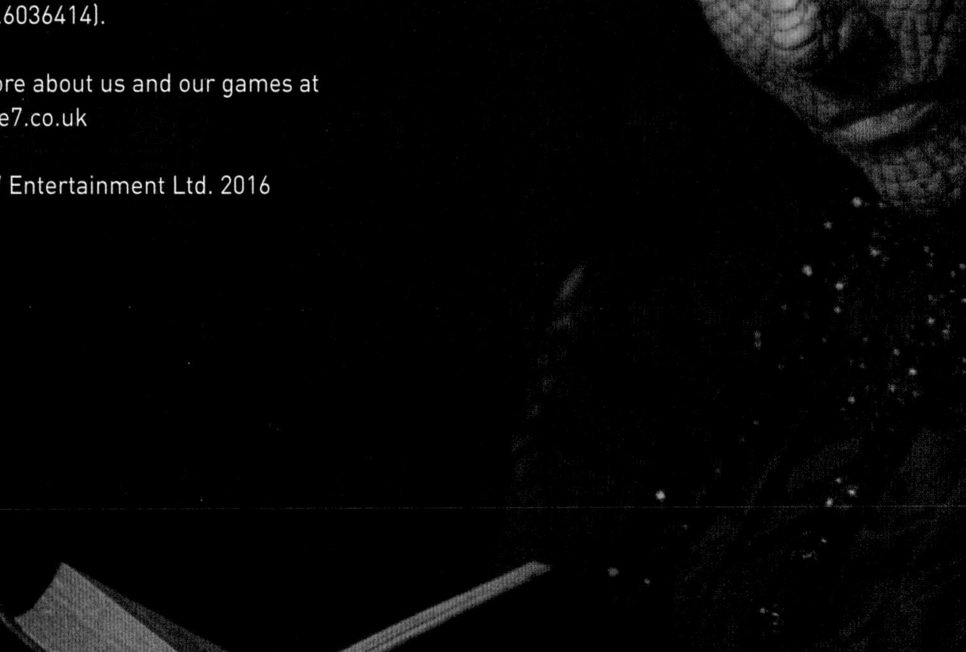

Printed by: Standartų Spaustuvė, www.standart.lt, Vilnius, Lithuania.

CONTENTS

INTRODUCTION 4

AN AGE OF MARVELS 6
The Late Victorian Age 7
What Do You Mean by "Victorian"? 8
A Matter of Class 8
Women and the Home 9
Grand Designs 10
Marvels and Mysteries 10
Famous Personalities of the Age 11
Queen Victoria and the Royal Family 11
Artists 11
Writers 12
Scientists 13
Explorers 14
Social Reformers 15
History Through a Different Lens 16
Everything Changes and Nothing is as it Seems 18
Evoke the Era 18
Alien Mindsets 19
Room to Breathe 19
A (Secret) History of the Late Victorian Age 20
The Doctor's Victorian Adventures 29
Dark Shadows 29
Adventures in the Victorian Age 31
Victorian Adventures...in Space! 33

THE PATERNOSTER'S GUIDE TO LONDON 34
Dividing the City 35
Central London 36
East London 38
West London 40
South London 42
North London 43
Paternoster Irregulars 46
Professor Augusta Barlow 46
Nurse Janet Blackwood 47
Lord Alexander Fitzstephen 48
Gabrielle Fitzstephen 48
Ada Gillyflower 49
Inspector Tobias Gregson 50
Madame Horowitz 51
Karratuddoranna 51
Dame Regina Smythe 52
Franklin Tuttle 53
The Prime Minister 53
The Principal Private Secretary 54
Rogues' Gallery 55
The Artful Dodger 55
Miss Annie 56
Leper Hall 57
Alice Shield 57
Hester Biggs 59
Korval 60
The Napoleon of Crime 60
Mister Steele 62
Miss Lovelace 63
Chessmen 64
Cybershade 64
The Revenant Reverend 65
Scarlett Valentin 66
Antoine Petit 68
Rollo Ford 68
The Torchwood Institute 69
Lady Isobel MacLeish 70
Sir Edward Tolliver 70
Allan Quincy Riddell 71
Rhona Austen 72
The Borad 73
Dr Karfelov 75
Josephine 75

VICTORIAN ADVENTURES 77
Your Own Paternoster Gang 78
Creating Paternoster Characters 79
Alien Characters 82
New Traits 83
Devices and Gadgets 85
The Doctor's Victorian Companions 86
The Paternoster Gang 87
The Further Adventures of Jackson Lake 88
Jago and Litefoot Investigate 89
The Many Faces of Clara Oswald 89
A Victorian Out of Time 90

THE PATERNOSTER CAMPAIGN 91
It's a Team Effort 92
How Capable? 92
Temporally Tethered 93
A Victorian Conceit 94
Greater Latitude with Conceits 95
Creating Paternoster Adventures 96
Aliens in London 96
The Steampunk Lens 97
The Art of Deduction, or Lack Thereof 97

A STUDY IN FLAX 99
Adventure Synopsis 100
The Zygma Experiments 100
1. Queen Guinevere is Missing 101
2. Pounding the Cobblestones 104
3. The House of Me 106
4. Heist Clean-up 108
5. Case Unexpectedly Closed? 111
6. Temporal Workshop 112
Ending the Adventure 115

APPENDIX: CHARACTER SHEETS 116
Madame Vastra 117
Jenny Flint 118
Strax 119
Jackson Lake 120
Rosita Farisi 121
Henry Gordon Jago 122
Professor Litefoot 123
Clara Oswin Oswald 124
Victoria Waterfield 125

INDEX 126

Paternoster Investigations is about the Doctor's adventures in the Victorian era with the Paternoster Gang. We present all manner of detail on the sort of characters you can create and the adventures you might have in the fog covered streets of old London town. Madame Vastra and her companions will take you on a journey across the city, showing you the sights and sounds, and introducing you to an array of villains and contacts. We lay out the Victorian age in simple terms, giving the Gamemaster a style guide for creating adventures, be they visits from time travellers or campaigns led by alien adventurers. **Paternoster Investigations** is divided into five distinct chapters:

An Age of Marvels

Join us on a whistle-stop tour of the Victorian era as we introduce this time of change and revolution, along with a number of its movers and key moments. We also take a look at the Doctor's own adventures in the era.

The Paternoster Guide to London

The Paternoster Gang take you on a tour of the cobbled streets and alleys of London, as well as explain the harsh realities of crime, class and other features of the age. They will also show you a few of their hideouts and some of the more famous landmarks in the city. The chapter also describes an array of new villains and potential contacts to help create a web of intrigue.

Victorian Adventurers

This chapter is all about creating your own Victorian characters, whether they are about to embark on time-travelling adventures in the TARDIS or stay to fight aliens on the streets of London. The chapter also includes some of the Doctor's more memorable companions of the era, including the Paternoster Gang themselves, and fellow investigators like Jackson Lake and Jago and Litefoot.

The Paternoster Campaign

This chapter takes a look at creating Victorian campaigns, providing the Gamemaster with plentiful advice about running investigative games in the manner of Madame Vastra's sleuthing.

A Study in Flax

The final part of the book contains a complete adventure set in Paternoster London. The gang must investigate the mysterious disappearance of a flaxen-haired actress, stumbling upon a sinister alliance behind a series of abductions.

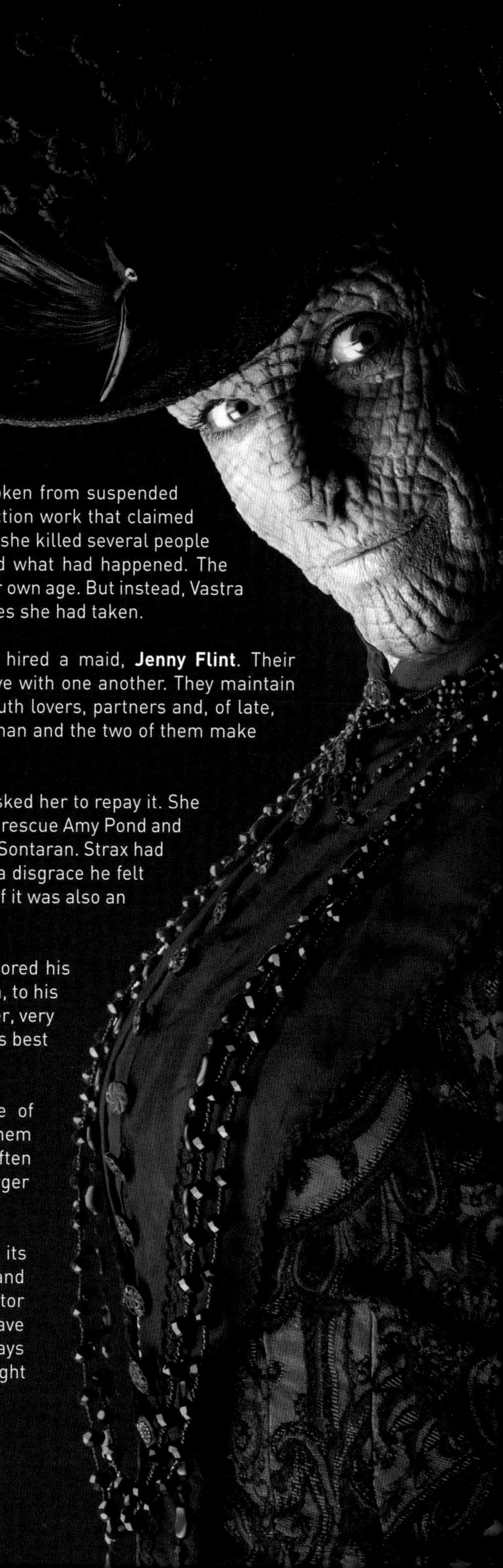

Appendix
The book is rounded off with ready-made character sheets for the Doctor's companions.

THE PATERNOSTER GANG

The Doctor can't be everywhere, all the time, and so an unusual band of heroes have been drawn together to fight crime on the streets of Victorian London. Together, they do their best to carry on the Doctor's work and keep the city safe from criminals, murderers and the occasional alien invasion – an event that is a lot more common than you might think.

This band of heroes is led by **Madame Vastra**, a Silurian warrior awoken from suspended animation by construction work on the London underground, construction work that claimed the lives of her brothers and sisters. Her first reaction was violent and she killed several people out of revenge until the Doctor found her. He helped her understand what had happened. The Doctor could have returned her to her slumber, or taken her back to her own age. But instead, Vastra decided to remain where she was to make amends for the innocent lives she had taken.

To help her with day-to-day life in this strange new world, Vastra hired a maid, **Jenny Flint**. Their relationship grew in ways neither of them expected, as they fell in love with one another. They maintain the pretence of lady and housemaid for propriety's sake, but are in truth lovers, partners and, of late, wives. Under Vastra's tuition, Jenny has become an expert swordswoman and the two of them make a deadly couple.

But Vastra always knew she owed the Doctor a debt, and one day he asked her to repay it. She and Jenny joined the battle at Demon's Run, where the Doctor fought to rescue Amy Pond and her child. Another member of this motley army was **Strax**, a disgraced Sontaran. Strax had been forced to become a nurse as a punishment for a loss of honour, a disgrace he felt keenly. So he was more than happy to join a glorious battle, especially if it was also an opportunity to repay a debt he owed the Doctor.

Strax believed he had died in the battle, a glorious final end that restored his honour. But with the help of Vastra and Jenny he was restored to health, to his great disappointment. Strax accepted Vastra's offer to become her butler, very much hoping it was a military position. Sadly, it was not, but he does his best to make it a warrior's career whenever possible.

Together, the gang investigate crimes in the city, especially those of unusual or alien provenance. The group's unique skills have gained them the attention of Scotland Yard and the city's police detectives. They often come to the house on Paternoster Row to ask for advice on the stranger cases they find.

Together, the Paternoster Gang have faced the Great Intelligence and its deadly servants, Mrs Gillyflower and Mister Sweet, a rampaging T-rex and the Clockwork Robots of the Half-face Man. They have brought the Doctor out of retirement and helped him recover from regeneration. They have stood against the shadow and prevailed. While the Doctor might not always be around, the Paternoster Gang stand ready to say to those who might come to Victorian London to do harm: "It is defended."

AN AGE OF MARVELS

AN AGE OF MARVELS

The Victorian age is an age of powerful new technology and sweeping social change. Great steam-powered factories claim thousands of souls to serve clattering looms and burning steel foundries. Fog and smoke lies thick on the city streets, shadows and strangers hiding in the gloom of gaslight. Dark and dangerous villains and monsters might lurk around any corner, looking to prey on the weak and vulnerable.

But there is more to the Victorian age than fog and despair. The industrial revolution has exploded with new technology and incredible advances appear at a seemingly daily rate. Talented engineers link the country together with rails and bridges. Brilliant scientists make discoveries and craft theories that shake society to the core. Mystics and magicians claim to hold the keys to the secrets of the universe.

The world is changing at breathtaking speed, and in the centre of the world is Britain, the leader of a vast mercantile empire. At the heart of the British Empire, London, the dark urban sprawl that has become the envy of the world. It is a city that offers any delight a visitor might ask for. Goods and services from around the world are drawn here by the power of Empire.

This is an age of science and magic, of wonders and horrors. But under the cover of new technology and strange people, aliens find it simple to hide their plans. To take control of London is to take control of Britain. To take control of Britain is to take control of the Earth.

This is an age the Doctor is all too familiar with. He has walked the streets of Whitechapel disguised as Sherlock Holmes, hidden away here as he mourned the loss of his best friend, and even chased a dinosaur through the streets wearing only a nightshirt. In his footsteps, as ever, have come companions and heroes who remain behind to carry on his work.

THE LATE VICTORIAN AGE

Before you begin to create your own adventures in the Victorian age, we should take a look at the era itself. But don't worry, we won't be listing oceans of dates and expecting you to sit a history test afterwards. The Victorian era is a fascinating place, a time of battle, revolution, innovation and excitement. But it is also a time of brutal labour, political trouble, imperial arrogance and oppression. To help you understand the world your characters are part of, we need to detail the setting.

In this book we'll be offering a rather broad description, choosing to focus on the aspects relevant to the sort of adventures the Doctor and the Paternoster Gang might have. Much like in an episode of Doctor Who, you don't need to get bogged down in historical detail; rather than worry about dates, you can easily default to just 'Victorian'. What really matters is capturing the style rather than historical detail of this complicated age.

As a Gamemaster you need to detail a London that 'feels' Victorian, even if some of the details aren't quite as the history books have them. With alien invasions, Clockwork Robots, rogue dinosaurs and giant cyborg killing machines stalking the streets, historical accuracy has already taken something of a beating. Follow the same cues in your own games, making it feel like an exciting adventure rather than a history lesson!

WHEN IS PATERNOSTER INVESTIGATIONS SET?

We presume that your Paternoster campaign is going to take place in the last decade of the Victorian era, but we leave it fuzzy as to exactly when so you can avoid getting bogged down in dates and times. In order to help you get a handle on easing off of historical accuracy, we've expressly set **Paternoster Investigations** in 189X, where the 'X' can stand in for any year in the last decade. We aren't particularly worried about whether an opera was performed in 1896 or a battle took place in 1894; if you need them to happen concurrently for your adventure to work, then they simply do.

WHAT DO WE MEAN BY "VICTORIAN"?

A lot of things tend to get labelled "Victorian" when someone just means "old". But it is easy to make that mistake; the era was long and society underwent a great many changes during that time. The world at the start of the era is very different from the world at the end of it.

The Victorian age begins in 1837 with the coronation of Queen Victoria. It ends with her death in 1901. The Regency era of Jane Austen precedes it, bringing the beginnings of change in social class and industry. It was followed by the Edwardian era, which builds on its social movements and technology with the Suffragettes and the rise of the motor car.

To give you an overview of the age, we can separate the era into three different rough divisions:

Early Victorian (1830s-1860s): The era of Charles Dickens, crinoline skirts and bonnets, new gas lighting, railway time and postage stamps. It is the Victorian era of Christmas cards, a time of transition between the pastoral Regency and the industrial Victorian. With industrialisation comes pollution, leading to the creation of new sewage systems in London.

Mid-Victorian (1860s-1880s): The age of penny farthings and electrical lighting. The gramophone and electric tram spearhead an array of new devices powered by electricity rather than gas and steam. The position of women changes dramatically.

Late Victorian (1880s-1901): The dark age of the era. The streets are full of smog and the industrial age is polluting everything. The shadows grow larger in reality and fiction; this is the age of Dracula, Jack the Ripper and Sherlock Holmes. Moving pictures are invented.

When it comes to running **Paternoster Investigations,** you don't need to worry about precise (or even imprecise) dates. Far better to capture the feel of the era with brief descriptions bordering on a pastiche than to get carried away with historical accuracy. This is the setting for a ***Doctor Who*** adventure, not a historical drama, after all.

A MATTER OF CLASS

Key to understanding the Victorian era is the importance of social class. There are three layers to society: upper class, middle class and lower or working class. Each is so different from one another that they might as well inhabit different worlds. Victorian society is not a meritocracy. What one can and cannot do is largely predetermined by birth. While those of a different class might marry, or the lower orders might gain acceptance among their betters, such cases are unusual; they are always met with suspicion at best, and horror, outrage and ostracism at worst.

The upper class make up a tiny fraction of the population, but control most of the wealth. They live in huge houses and wear beautiful clothes with servants waiting on their every whim. Their wealth is based on land and so they don't need to do any form of work. In fact, taking a job is a great disgrace. However, some find an occupation as a consultant for some expertise, an academic, scientist or philanthropist.

The upper class believes that they have 'innate breeding'; they are literally born to lead. They occupy most of the positions of power because it is assumed only they know what must be done. This gives them an arrogance beyond that of the wealthy privilege they enjoy.

But life for the upper class is as restrictive as it is comfortable. Barred from physical labour or any sort of career, they fill their days by visiting one another and organising social events. The days in between can be tedious in the extreme and lead them to focus on gossip and scandal to an almost obsessive degree.

The middle class are the entrepreneurs of society, the factory owners and professionals such as doctors, bankers and lawyers. They have carved out their position by dint of hard work and ruthless capitalism, and are the rising power in the age. For centuries, the upper class have tried to keep them out of their society by inventing complex forms of etiquette and dress. But many of the middle class have actually become wealthier than some of their 'betters'. They view the upper class as a bunch of useless dinosaurs, even though they envy their position. The middle class believe that they have truly built the British Empire, and will lead it to greatness.

The working or lower class is easily three times the size of the middle and upper classes combined. They are the poor and downtrodden who work hard to feed their families. Many are on the verge of starvation, except for the lucky ones who find good employment as servants for a wealthy family.

The lower class are often seen as expendable by the middle and upper classes, little more than fuel for the factories. However, the lower class also know they are the only people who actually get their hands dirty. Let the wealthy wax lyrical about building the Empire, it is the working class who did the real work. They have made Britain great with their labours, even if they rarely see the benefits. But for the working class, shifts are long and brutal. As it is expensive to bring the machines to a halt and stop production, many have lost fingers or limbs fixing jams or machine failures.

The minutiae of class and etiquette – while important to the Victorians – is not something that need overly worry you and your players. Paint a picture of the era with broad brushstrokes, occasionally adding in the odd interesting detail, rather than getting bogged down in class distinctions.

WOMEN AND THE HOME

In the late Victorian period, women have a significantly better deal than their forebears, but they are still far from equal. Before the Married Women's Property Act of 1870, women were not allowed to own anything at all, even their clothes. All they had belonged to their father, their husband or sometimes even their sons. It meant that they had little option but to do as they were told, as to be cast out was to be literally left with nothing. This is why many heiresses chose to remain unmarried. While in the late Victorian period they have control over their own finances to a greater degree, they still cannot vote and are denied from most positions of power.

The Victorian ideal of women was "the angel in the home". A pure and unassailable, virtuous creature of silence who bore children and kept the house in immaculate order. To the Victorian, the home was everything. They were not as prudish as commonly believed; never actually covering table legs for fear of impropriety. In fact, they were remarkably open to all manner of scandal as long as that scandal never left the house. "An Englishman's home is his castle" meant that within the walls of the home, for good or ill, anything goes.

Of course, the Doctor's companions invariably buck the trend no matter the era they hail from, and those joining him from the Victorian era are likely to be anything but subservient housewives.

GRAND DESIGNS

It would be impossible to catalogue the range of technological devices and advances that were made in the era. The beginning of the age was lit by candlelight, the middle by gaslight and the end by electrical light. New ideas appeared on almost a daily basis. Time itself changed; with the coming of the railways it was important that everyone was on the same schedule across the country, so a national system of standard timekeeping centred at Greenwich was created, one that eventually spread across the empire.

What stands out, though, are the vast engineering projects that remain today. The Victorians built extensive railways across the country, linking every part of the British Isles together and making excursions to the coast cheap and popular. New bridges and tunnels linked places no one thought possible. Huge steam ships like the SS Great Britain defied conventional thought that a vast ship made of iron would even float. London received a sewer system that turned 'the Great Stink' into a habitable city once more. The engineers dug even deeper to create a new underground railway. These projects were vast in their scope and only possible due to Britain's incredible wealth. Across the cities, factories sprung up, full of steam-powered machines capable of creating mass-produced goods. What had taken weeks to make by hand could now be made in a day with these huge and tireless machines. People left the countryside in droves to find work in the city, leaving the countryside bare. The country began to suffer as farms lacked the labour they required, but still the polluted cities claimed more folk.

MARVELS AND MYSTERIES

So how does all this fit into the Doctor's adventures? Surely, technology so advanced to appear magical will stand out. How will people fail to notice aliens walking the streets? Quite the opposite, in fact, for the wonders of the Victorian age makes it so much easier for all this strangeness to pass unnoticed. With so much new technology and so many different people coming to the heart of the Empire daily, the strange and unusual rarely gets a second glance. This is an age of so many marvels that a few more added to the mix are oddly commonplace.

Technology is the marvel of the age, but the scientific method is a new idea. Before this era, scientists were referred to as "natural philosophers" who mused on the mechanics of existence. But, as the Victorian age dawned, several academics coined the term science. This was not an age for guesswork but for empirical thought and observation. Science was not an educated guess but objective fact reached by experimentation.

The problem, however, was that it was very unclear what was science and what was fiction. Did faeries exist? Was magic just another force scientists had yet to quantify? Could mediums reach into the realm of the dead? Could ghosts leave this realm to walk the earth? All these things were open to experimentation, but no one had yet proved or disproved them as truth. So any technology, no matter how strange or seemingly magical, was considered science until proved otherwise. The Victorians would think little of a strange man tinkering with a blue box that was bigger on the inside. It was simply a form of science they did not yet understand.

The same applied to people. The Victorian era was the first time people really began to explore the world. London drew many of the subjects of the new British Empire to its streets looking for a new life. People from all parts of the world found a home here, and to the British they appeared strange and alien in many ways. With strange rumours and travellers' tales adding to the mythology, even a green-skinned lizard might appear to be just another visitor from some far away land.

FAMOUS PERSONALITIES OF THE AGE

The Victorian age gave birth to an array of driven and talented people, men and women who were the driving force behind the advances and changes of the century. There were new movements in art, science, social change and exploration. You could easily fill a book just listing their names, so instead we'll offer you a brief introduction to some of the more noted individuals of the age, such as you might be given should you meet them at a social occasion or that the Doctor might already know – handy for when he bumps into one of them while being chased by a Werewolf.

QUEEN VICTORIA AND THE ROYAL FAMILY

Queen Victoria is the most renowned person of the age, and her family life had more than its fair share of drama. From a very young age she was the heir presumptive, and her mother had her own designs on the throne. She did her best to control and restrict the young Victoria in the hopes of breaking her will. But upon taking the throne in 1837, aged only 18, she banished her mother from her sight.

In 1840 Victoria married Albert of Saxe-Coburg. Their marriage might have been an arranged one (to a certain degree by Victoria herself) but it was a very happy one. They had nine children together: Victoria, Albert, Alice, Alfred, Helena, Louise, Arthur, Leopold and Beatrice. Albert died of Typhoid fever in 1861; Victoria was devastated, and entered into a period of mourning she never really recovered from. She turned from an intelligent and dedicated Queen, into a dour recluse whose presence made the weddings of some of her younger children seem more like funerals.

By 189X, the Queen is rarely, if ever, seen in public. She has, however, returned to most of her duties as Empress. For most public appearances and social gatherings, the Queen is represented by one of her children. Princess Beatrice works as her unofficial secretary and Princess Louise often 'stands in' for her mother. While the Queen may be difficult to gain an audience with, her children are comparatively easy to encounter. Most of them attend high society occasions, often accompanied by their high-ranking spouses. If the characters are invited to a formal and highly ranked affair, they may well encounter a member of the royal family.

ARTISTS

Art remains a very popular part of Victorian culture. It still has the power to shock and impress and many artists have shaken the foundations of the establishment with their paintings. While the lower classes don't get the time to go to exhibitions, the upper and middle classes are frequent patrons of the art. There are many art exhibitions organised throughout the season where artists show new works to the public. Several different artistic movements are also popular; the impressionist style from France (Monet, Cézanne, Degas and Renoir in particular) is the latest craze.

Most artists, even the most famous, attend the showings of their paintings, and many have become renowned society figures. However, the more controversial artists can be quite hard to locate, especially if their work has drawn anger from the crowds. Augustus Egg in particular causes much unrest with his triptych *Past and Present*, which details the breakdown of the Victorian home. Frank Holl (himself a royal portraitist) draws attention to the inequality of the lower class with works such as *Newgate – Committed for Trial*.

Two artists of particular note are James Tissot and Gustave Doré. Both came to London to paint and draw scenes from everyday Victorian life. Their work forms a 'photo-journal' of the era and are highly recommended as a resource for the Gamemaster looking to paint a picture of the era.

William Morris (1834-1896)
Morris began his career as an artist but moved into textiles after an apprenticeship among the Pre-Raphaelites. He had as much talent for business as he had for art; his interior designs, wallpapers and textiles became the vogue for most of the Victorian era. In 189X Morris is an old man but he remains active and robust until his death from Tuberculosis in 1896. He is a staunch activist, anti-imperialist and social reformer as well as an atheist. It is more likely that the characters will come across him in one of these roles than as an artist!

William Powell Frith (1819-1909)
One of the most renowned artists of the day is William Powell Frith. His huge populated landscape scenes full of detail show the bustle of Victorian life. He has a somewhat curious family life. After having 12 children with his wife, he marries his mistress (who lived a mile down the road) upon his wife's death. Frith is an outspoken critic of the Pre-Raphaelites, eschewing their idealistic beauty for a more realistic portrait of Victorian life. He widely exhibits his work, and is a renowned raconteur, making him a popular guest at social occasions. His most famous works are *The Crossing Sweeper, Derby Day, A Private View at the Royal Academy* and *The Railway Station*.

WRITERS

Growing levels of literacy have made the novel a popular pastime, although they remain comparatively expensive. The early part of the century brought the bohemian controversy of Lord Byron and the romantic poets, as well as Mary Shelley's unsettling Gothic work *Frankenstein*. Regency writers like Jane Austen set the stage for novels as social commentary, proving that the novel could do more than just tell a story. Poetry is also very popular, with Alfred Lord Tennyson (Poet Laureate for most of Victoria's reign) and Christina Rossetti (whose brother Dante founded the Pre-Raphaelite movement) among a long list of renowned poets.

Robert Louis Stevenson (1850-1894)
This Scottish novelist, essayist and travel writer is best known for *Treasure Island, Kidnapped* and *Dr Jekyll and Mr Hyde*. While a prolific writer, Stevenson was dogged with ill health and travelled often in the search of a healthier climate. As an active member of the literary set, characters might meet him at any of London's more academic clubs, or they might encounter him during his travels to exotic parts of the world.

CHARLES DICKENS (1812-1870)

By the time of **Paternoster Investigations**, Charles Dickens is sadly dead, but his legacy remains. His work was extremely popular, with most of his novels published episodically in small and affordable journals. He was a master of the 'cliff hanger' and had most of London desperate for the next instalment. Even in his later years, Dickens remained fit and healthy, continuing to write and tour the country performing readings from his work. In a campaign set earlier in the century, the characters might meet Dickens at one of these many performances (just as the Doctor did – see **The Unquiet Dead** in ***The Ninth Doctor Sourcebook***).

Lewis Carroll (1832-1898)
The writer of *Alice's Adventures in Wonderland* and *Through the Looking Glass* was actually named Charles Lutwidge Dodgson. However, Dodgson was really more of a dilettante than a novelist. He pursued several gentlemanly hobbies, and was renowned as a mathematician and a photographer. He was a great friend of the well-placed Liddell family, whose youngest daughter Alice proved the inspiration for his novels. The Liddells had connections with the highest in society and Alice was rumoured to briefly be a paramour of Queen Victoria's youngest son Leopold. Dodgson might turn up in any number of places, from academia to royal occasions.

Arthur Conan Doyle (1859-1930)
The author of the renowned Sherlock Holmes stories was himself a trained physician. However, he stopped practising full time once his writing career took off. He was a keen sportsman and political campaigner too, and wrote works supporting the Boer War and stood for parliament as a Liberal Unionist. While Sherlock Holmes (a character clearly based on Madame Vastra and her adventures – see pg. 20) often found mundane solutions for his most mysterious cases, Doyle was fascinated with the unseen world. He joined the Freemasons and the Society for Psychical Research (see pg. 27). His investigations might lead him to cross paths with the characters, especially if they have some apparently supernatural traits themselves.

Herbert George Wells (1866-1946)
Young Herbert Wells might have remained a teacher had it not been for a chance encounter with the Doctor (see **Timelash** in ***The Sixth Doctor Sourcebook***).

Taken to an alien world and thrown forwards and backwards in time, young Herbert was inspired enough to write a novel, *The Time Machine*, in 1895. He followed this work with several classics, most notably *The Island of Dr Moreau* (1896), *The Invisible Man* (1897) and *The War of the Worlds* (1898). He won the Nobel Prize for literature no less than four times, and along with Jules Verne is regarded as one of the fathers of science fiction. Given his adventure with the Doctor, one might begin to wonder if his novels are entirely works of fiction. Even without his experiences with strange concepts and technology, Wells might still be a wise councillor when it comes to such things in Victorian London.

SCIENTISTS

In an age of science, the list of innovators and inventors is vast. However, such people are often difficult to meet outside academic settings. Most prefer to remain in their laboratories and workshops, but a few are called upon to debate their findings among other scientists. Others are forced to defend their work from the church and establishment. While the era is an age of science, Christianity remains a powerful force whose tenets are still considered immutable facts. Where conflict occurs between established belief and new research, the arguments often become passionate and uncompromising.

Charles Darwin (1809-1882)
Darwin is credited as the father of evolutionary theory, although others (such as Alfred Wallace) were also working on similar research. His ideas proved highly controversial, directly challenging the Bible. Darwin's contention that humans were descended from ape-like ancestors caused ridicule even in academic circles. Darwin was unable to defend his ideas in public debate due to ill health, but he was a fervent letter writer and engaged with his detractors as often as possible.

Isambard Kingdom Brunel (1806-1859)
If the Victorian age of engineering has a father, it is surely Isambard Kingdom Brunel. He built the Great Western Railway and many supposedly impossible bridges to ensure trains could travel the length and breadth of Britain. In later life he turned to the sea, designing the SS *Great Western* and the SS *Great Britain*, which proved the efficiency of propeller-driven ships over paddle wheels. His last creation, the SS *Great Eastern* was designed for long-distance travel to India and was the largest ship built. Brunel died just before its launch.

Charles Babbage (1791-1871)
Babbage is considered the conceptual inventor of the programmable computer. While some of his designs were built, they were never completed. What might

have been had he finished his work? Might it have been that a time traveller from the future or an alien have stopped him?

Ada Lovelace (1815-1852)
Ada Lovelace was the illegitimate daughter of the infamous Lord Byron. Her mother studiously promoted Ada's mathematical talents to steer her away from becoming an artist like her father. She corresponded with Babbage and Faraday and created algorithms for use in programming Babbage's theoretical machines. As the first computer programmer, her talents might allow her to understand any computer code system, perhaps even those from the future.

Joseph Lister (1827-1912)
This British surgeon championed the idea of sterility during operations. Surgeons before this time rarely even washed their hands between patients. Lister also created a carbolic spray for use in surgery to fight infection.

Louis Pasteur (1822-1895)
Louis Pasteur is credited with the invention of the vaccine and the study of germs and diseases. He is the foremost immunologist of the time.

Mary Anning (1799-1847)
Mary Anning was an early palaeontologist and naturalist, and discovered several major complete dinosaur fossils. As a woman, she was not eligible to join the main scientific organisations and much of her work was uncredited. Madame Vastra may well have an interest in her studies.

Gregor Mendel (1822-1884)
Mendel was the founder of the science of genetics, establishing the rules and systems of heredity. What he might have concluded had he come across alien DNA?

EXPLORERS

With new wealth has come the time and resources for British explorers to mount expeditions to the most remote corners of the world. What they might find there is sometimes not as interesting as what they might bring back with them...

Richard Francis Burton (1821-1890)
Burton risked his life for the sake of adventure and exploration on more than one occasion. Most famously he travelled to Mecca in 1853, which was forbidden under pain of death for non-Muslims. It took him two years to build an Arabian identity to allow him to infiltrate the city. In his later years he settled down and wrote several books on his experiences. He would be a valuable contact should the characters come across something strange and previously unseen in their investigations.

Isabella Bird (1831-1904)
The outspoken daughter of a clergyman, Isabella Bird became a renowned naturalist, explorer and photographer. Despite ill health she travelled to

Australia and explored her way across most of Asia. Her achievements lead her to become the first woman to be allowed to join the Royal Geographical Society in 1892. She is one of the foremost British experts on Asian lore, but if you need to speak to her you had best be quick as she begins to plan her next adventure as soon as she gets home.

David Livingstone (1813-1873)
Born to lower class beginnings in Scotland, David Livingstone rose to become one of the foremost explorers of Africa. He led expeditions into the interior of the continent, famously losing contact with the outside world for six years. He was 'found' in an African village by journalist Henry Stanley who famously quipped, "Dr Livingstone, I presume?"

SOCIAL REFORMERS

In an age of new invention and feats of civil engineering, many people are working to change the inequalities in society. Some, such as Harriet Martineau (often cited as the first female sociologist and an early feminist) were even favourites of Queen Victoria. Pressure groups finally won women the right to own property after marriage and the proposal to allow women the vote has been heard in parliament, even though this time it was voted down. But many social issues remain, most especially among the poor and the working class. Successes in social reform include the creation of a police force by Robert Peel (hence 'Bobbies' or 'Peelers') and the work of prison reformer Elizabeth Fry.

Florence Nightingale (1820-1910)
Nightingale is best known for her contribution to modern nursing during the Crimean War (1853-1856). She realised that keeping the wounded in unsanitary conditions with little support or care was not doing them any good. While Strax likely agrees with her theories and practices, it is unlikely they share the same opinion about frontal assaults. In her later years, Florence works in hospital management and many of the nurses she trained can be found working in London's hospitals. Her connections across the medical profession are second to none.

Mary Seacole (1805-1881)
A skilled nurse of Caribbean and Scottish descent, Mary served during epidemics in the Caribbean and Panama before coming to the Crimea. During her time there she set up a British hospital and was a contemporary of Florence Nightingale. However, her achievements did not receive as much credit due to her Caribbean descent. In the late Victorian era she returned to London, offering aid to those who wish to remain anonymous...

Elizabeth Garrett Anderson (1836-1917)
Elizabeth was the first British woman to become a doctor, a title she had to fight long and hard to gain. She had to study as both a nurse and an apothecary to get close enough to attain membership of the British Medical Association. She remained the only female member for 19 years, as the society quickly closed the loophole that had allowed her to join their number!

Luckily, Elizabeth had the help and support of 'the Kensington Society' a small but growing group of women who meet to discuss academic subjects not traditionally considered appropriate for women. No doubt Madame Vastra is a member herself, and the society may well form a vital part of the Paternoster Irregulars.

HISTORY THROUGH A DIFFERENT LENS

We presume that your Paternoster campaign is going to take place in the last decade of the Victorian era. Whichever year you chose, it is vitally important that you understand which Prime Minister is running Parliament, what the exact global geo-political situation is like during that year, and the exact movements of key pivotal artistic and social figures residing in London at that moment. You need to be precise and historically accurate if you want to run a successful Paternoster adventure. Well, not quite. Not at all, actually. Not even a little bit.

You see, claiming that you need to be historically accurate is predicated on a false premise, and that is that the Doctor's adventures through space and time always match with recorded history. As we all know, records can be lost, doctored, forgotten, misremembered or even rewritten. Alien creatures, from the lone sightseer to the full invasion force, constantly interact with our own history with none of it ever being recorded, at least, not in our version of the past. As the Doctor and the Paternoster Gang have shown time and time again, history is mutable and everything can change, even when you remember it differently. It's no different to the way events actually happen to you, and the way you put your own spin on it when recalling it at the pub with your friends.

In short, there is nothing preventing you from presenting the Victorian world of the Paternoster Gang in the way that you want, whether the events that you present are concurrent, happened a few years earlier, or are supposed to happen in the future. There's also nothing stopping you from scorching half of the East End thanks to a Dalek invasion, or having Britain and Germany on the brink of a great war a couple of decades early. It's your campaign, and first and foremost you need to present an enjoyable setting for your Paternosters to muck about in, conventions be damned!

To better illustrate this concept let's look at two extended periods of the Doctor's adventures on Earth, most notably his exile on Earth in his third incarnation, more popularly known as the 'UNIT Era,' and Earth's first decade in the aftermath of the Time War, which we'll call the 'Modern Era.' We'll start with the Modern Era first, as that is the most recent and most familiar to our own.

Or is it? Presumably we're all familiar with Earth's history over the last decade, but during the Doctor's adventures a lot of things have happened that we've never seen in our world, such as the faked alien first contact by the Slitheen, the destruction of 10 Downing Street, Earth's hijacking by the Daleks, the motorists' installation of ATMOS, the Adipose weight loss craze, and the murders of the British Prime Minister and the American President-Elect (not to mention the fact that another Prime Minister turned out to be the Master), along with several alien invasions. We've also seen people from our world using incredible technologies, both Earth-made and alien, that we don't have in our own world, such as alien ship-destroying lasers and flying fortresses.

And yet, with all of these differences, we never fail to recognise the time and place as our Earth when the TARDIS lands on it. There is enough familiarity for us to overlook, or even accept, the strange and out of place. We understand that the Doctor, his allies, and his enemies leave their mark on our world whenever they interact with it.

The UNIT Era is even a bit further afield. Thanks to the dating protocols of classified dossiers, we aren't even sure when the Doctor was exiled to Earth – a case can be made for the tail end of the 1960s, somewhere in the 1970s, or even into the 1980s.

In some instances, it even seems to be a post-Cold War era, which from our perspective would push the dates into the late 1980s and even the early 1990s!

It's an era where the United Kingdom has a thriving space programme, the launch codes for the world's nuclear arsenal, and an armed and quasi-independent international military force specifically tasked to deal with alien threats in the aftermath of two invasions, one local to London, and one worldwide (the Great Intelligence and the Cybermen, respectively).

And yet again, when we think about the period of the Doctor's exile with UNIT, we have little trouble imagining it taking place somewhen in the 1970s, even with all of the inconsistencies, alien invasions, alternative Prime Ministers, and strange technologies that don't exactly correspond with our recollections and records of that time period. Even today, if the player characters hopped into a TARDIS in 2016 and travelled back to the mid-1970s, we'd expect them to bump into Brigadier Lethbridge-Stewart and his team, or at the very least have them referenced.

The lessons of these two eras can also be applied to the Paternoster Era. Paternoster London is clearly the 1890s, but there are key differences, such as memories of a Cyber-King in the Thames, a dinosaur traipsing through central London and killer snowmen in the Paternoster present.

In short, it's OK to have the Paternoster Gang run roughshod over a Victorian era that's been touched by the Doctor's – and their own – adventures, without having to slavishly adhere to the specifics of history. So, when putting together adventures in the Paternoster era, here are a few things to keep in mind.

EVERYTHING CHANGES AND NOTHING IS AS IT SEEMS

First and foremost, remember that everything changes. The Last Great Time War caused ripples across the universe and, as indicated by its name, it was not the only temporal conflict in history. Similarly, the Doctor, other Time Lords, Earth Time Agents, the Daleks, the Cybermen, and several other species and factions have meddled with time. The events that we believe to be true are only the most recent versions of them – at any moment, time can be rewritten and we'll remember it differently. On the other hand, time is resilient. While various temporal forces often change the details, time generally flows along the course it was meant to. After all, only major changes stand out and often attract the attention of those who feel compelled to fix it, while little changes tend to go unnoticed. In other words, a lone Zygon travelling through the streets of Victorian London may be overlooked, but a Zygon invasion that leaves the city in flames and overthrows the government is going to attract attention.

In addition, there's a lot that the history books get wrong, whether due to careful editing to hide the truth or a time traveller's attempt to 'fix' things. Our history books consider the Trojan War to be a myth, much less give the Doctor credit for coming up with the Trojan Horse. Robin Hood was both engineered and relegated to myth, and the Doctor was partially responsible for the Great Fire of London. HG Wells was inspired to write his science fiction stories based on an excursion through time, and Charles Dickens planned to alert the world to the presence of aliens just before he died. Still, with all of this, history remains familiar.

So what does this mean for your Paternoster adventures? Not only do you not need to worry about getting details correct, but even if you make a mistake it might not actually be a mistake – it's just the course history took before the next time ripple! Conversely, even if you get things 'right,' it's only accurate until another alien or temporal – or both! – intervention makes a change. In other words, plan your adventures based on what 'feels' right and is the most fun for your players!

EVOKE THE ERA

The reason why UNIT Era and Modern Era adventures work so well in spite of all the differences with our world is because they still strongly evoke their respective eras. So long as everything looks like it's the 1970s or the 2000s in broad strokes, then nobody's going to fixate on the small details. What's important is that you get the overall look and feel right so that your players' characters recognise and understand how to interact with the world.

Whether or not your players are historical scholars, they all probably have some idea of what 'Victorian London' should look like. It may be Sherlock Holmes, which is concurrent, or it may be Charles Dickens, which is not, but overall the differences between 1870s and 1890s London aren't going to mean much to them. So long as men are wearing top hats and waistcoats and women enjoy afternoon tea while their sons fight in some far-flung land for the British Empire, the players aren't going to worry too much about whether Bram Stoker's *Dracula* has been released yet or whether it's proper for an English gentleman to wear a bowler hat in 1895.

ALIEN MINDSETS

Most of the Paternoster Gang and their associates have one thing in common: they don't belong. Whether they're intelligent reptiles from Earth's distant pass, alien clone warriors, or simply humans with more modern sensibilities, they perceive the Victorian world around them with a mixture of awe and horror. They may find some of the particulars fascinating, such as its technological breakthroughs, genteel nature (at least amongst the upper classes), social customs and courting rituals, while they may find others quite appalling, such as low wages, dangerous working conditions, attitudes towards women and minorities, and rampant imperialism. Quite often they're baffled as to why the locals put up with it, much less fight against it.

As a Gamemaster, this is a very useful tool. Your players, like the Paternosters they're playing, are grounded in the early 21st century, where we've abandoned – unfortunately not entirely – the prejudices and inequities of the past. When you present something awful, your Paternosters should react to it like you'd hope your players would. Not only should they refuse to accept certain things because they're Victorian, but they should also have the same level of disconnect and amazement as the players.

If your players are unfamiliar with and baffled by the etiquette that they need to follow at a dinner party, then it's not exactly a stretch to have Madame Vastra or Strax also seem baffled by it. Nor would they feel any discomfort in doing things quite unheard of in the 1890s, such as two women in love getting married to each other, because it's simply not an issue for them.

ROOM TO BREATHE

If you want your players to embrace their alien-ness in the setting, then you have to give them room to breathe and explore it. The quickest way to stop such exploration cold is to lower the boom whenever it happens. Yes, the Victorian era was very paternalistic and patronising towards women (in spite of being ruled by a queen), but it wouldn't be much of an adventure if doors kept shutting in Madame Vastra's face and Strax couldn't get the time of day from anyone above the lower class.

While part of the fun in playing in the Victorian era is to highlight the peculiarities and subvert them, you'll want to dial down the reactions of the people surrounding your characters. Aberrant behaviours and social faux pas should be met with confused expressions and whispered disapproval; harsher reactions and measures should only be bestowed on the adventure's villains.

In the same vein, characters who are truly alien in appearance should be regarded as having a 'peculiar look' rather than outed as alien, so long as they make some pretence at disguising or justifying their appearance. In other words, it's enough to shine a light on the characters for their strange behaviours; you shouldn't beat them over the head with how 'wrong' they're acting.

In fact, you'll want to encourage your players to actively subvert expectations and even reward them with Story Points when they do so. There's much fun to be had with Madame Vastra being the smartest person in the room (while perhaps unnerving a gentleman by remarking how delicious he looks!) or Strax going overboard when advocating violent action in polite company. Much of the fun in a Paternoster campaign is to be had in these over-the-top moments – you'll definitely want to encourage your players to keep them coming!

BE INTERNALLY CONSISTENT

So now that we've given you licence to disregard history and Victorian attitudes, you might be wondering how to apply this to a Paternoster adventure without things devolving into absolute chaos. The answer is actually quite simple: be internally consistent. So long as you don't contradict yourself when plotting an adventure, things should turn out fine.

If you've decided, for example, that Bram Stoker's *Dracula* is on a character's bookshelf earlier in the campaign, then you can't have Stoker draw inspiration from a Paternoster mystery in a later adventure. Similarly, if you've introduced Jackson Lake to the characters then Scotland Yard detectives likely won't be baffled if they come across Cyber-technology – it's been seen before.

Don't forget to be internally consistent with reactions as well. If you've been letting an alien character get away with covering her face with a veil for two scenes and then have someone out her for using "such a ridiculous disguise", then you aren't being consistent. Similarly, if you allow Jenny access to areas outside her social class in early adventures, then she should be able to expect to continue to do so in later adventures. Inconsistency only frustrates players and slows things down while they reconsider every action.

One last note on internal consistency – remember how we discussed time ripples and the like above? These tend to work best outside the duration of a particular campaign. Nothing will frustrate the players more than you rewriting their adventures – and invalidating all of the decisions they made – by having someone go back in time and change things. This is not to say that you can't – there are excellent adventures to be had revolving around someone heading back in time – but you need to tread carefully to ensure that your players go along with the premise rather than be frustrated by it!

A (SECRET) HISTORY OF THE LATE VICTORIAN AGE

While time is certainly mutable and Gamemasters shouldn't feel constrained by the precise timing of historical events, **Paternoster Investigations** still takes place in what is recognisably London in the 1890s. Certain key events that happened in and around that time can be used as fodder for your adventures, even if you have to massage the dates a bit. Thus, while we list events that happened by year here, you can certainly decide that they take place in 189X instead! (See pg. 8 for more about dates.)

This is not an exhaustive list of yearly events; those listed here are merely intended to be springboards for ideas to create your own Paternoster adventures. As such, each event has notes to help you reshape and incorporate it into the course of a campaign.

1887 – THE GOLDEN JUBILEE

While a bit early for the Paternoster timeline, this year has special significance for it, as it marks the publication of the first story about the detective who might well have been modelled after Madame Vastra (and, likely to some extent, on the Doctor as well, as Scotland Yard has documented his help with a rather peculiar case involving giant rats and the Chinese tong).

The Birth of the Great Detective

This year marks the publication of the very first story involving Sherlock Holmes, *A Study in Scarlet*. Given the similarities between Mr Holmes and Madame Vastra, it is possible that Sir Arthur Conan Doyle was inspired by the Doctor and Madame Vastra to create the character (how would the Doctor feel about being relegated to the equivalent of Vastra's

'Watson'?). If you are starting the campaign early in the Paternoster Gang's career, then this is an excellent place to start, introducing not only Doyle but Jenny to the Great Detective who becomes her spouse!

Alternatively, it's possible that Doyle wasn't inspired by Vastra at all but merely noted the parallels once they'd met. Perhaps their adventure together shakes him and prompts the author to kill his creation in *The Final Problem*. On a lighter note, it's also possible that Doyle meets Vastra in 189X after having ended Holmes' life, and his getting caught up in Paternoster adventures is what inspires him to resurrect his most famous character in a few years.

Doyle's stories about Sherlock Holmes are a bountiful source of adventure seeds for your own Paternoster adventures, especially if you give them an alien twist. There are other detectives in the same vein as Holmes who you can use for inspiration as well – perhaps two of the players' own duo inspires GK Chesterton to reimagine them as Father Brown and his reformed criminal associate M Hercule Flambeau in the early 1900s!

Echoing the Golden Jubilee

Unless you are setting your **Paternoster Investigations** campaign at the beginning of Madame Vastra's career as a great detective, you might want to move Queen Victoria's Golden Jubilee forward in time to 189X (or her Diamond Jubilee back in time a little).

The Golden Jubilee hosted dozens of monarchs, heads of state and countless other prestigious guests. Should a villain or alien wish to hatch a plan that causes the most damage, gathering scores of world leaders in one room for a banquet is practically gift-wrapping an adventure for you!

The Irish Question

The question of Ireland is one that haunts Great Britain throughout the 19th century. For centuries Ireland was divided both politically and religiously. This was exacerbated in the 1801 Act of Union, which fully integrated Ireland with Great Britain and put it under the direct control of the British Parliament in London.

Adding to this was the Great Famine in the middle of the century, which only furthered tensions between Irish tenant farmers and their landlords and led to an increase both in Irish nationalism and agitation for home rule. An illustration of this tension took place on 13th November, when tens of thousands of protesters were met by police and soldiers in Trafalgar Square – hundreds were arrested and scores injured by the trampling of cavalry horses.

The troubles with Ireland are never far from one's thoughts in London and Scotland Yard has a branch dedicated to monitoring the activities of those associated with Irish republicanism. Whenever an anarchist or other terrorist attack takes place many presume that the Irish are responsible and those with suspected ties are immediately questioned.

Needless to say this only increases tensions, and a savvy alien criminal or vanguard can tap into this tension in order to gain local support or to use as a cover for their activities.

1888 – A CITY GRIPPED BY FEAR

1888 is an interesting year in Earth history, as it is marked by the return of the Gallifreyan living metal construct known as Nemesis and its influence always brings destruction. In Germany, two emperors die in quick succession, a blizzard in America's heartland leaves 235 dead – many children walking home from school – and, of course, London is plunged into fear over a mysterious serial killer who is preying on women.

This year is also notable for the establishment of the Isis-Urania Temple, which, unlike most other 'gentlemen's clubs,' was open to women as equal members.

The Silver Nemesis

The validium statue known as Nemesis was launched into space by the Doctor after keeping it out of the hands of Lady Peinforte, dabbler in black magic, in 1638. It became a comet that orbits the Earth, coming closest to it once every 25 years. The Nemesis' influence always brings death and destruction; its next two passes are on the eves of the World Wars, while its pass in 1963 coincided with the death of American President John F. Kennedy and very nearly plunged the Earth into a Third World War.

By those standards, however, the Nemesis' pass in 1888 seems rather insignificant. While Jack the Ripper is notorious, his crimes hardly threaten to plunge the world into chaos. So what did the Nemesis really do or, perhaps more accurately, how was it stopped? If you are setting your Paternoster campaign a little earlier, then it's possible that the Nemesis was thwarted by the timely intervention of your players!

It's possible that the Nemesis merely planted seeds in 1888 that only see fruition in 189X, just as it will show up a year before things get really hot in the World Wars. Whether or not this is connected to the truth about Jack the Ripper (see below) is unknown. Given the amount of Cyber-technology lying about in London during this period it's possible that a remaining Cyberman – even Mister Steele (see pg. 62) – may have felt the Nemesis' presence and is making plans to acquire it. Given that the validium is only a few years away in orbit then it's possible that a spacecraft could catch up with it (the Cybermen ultimately do catch up with Nemesis in 1988; perhaps it was at this time that they first discovered it?).

Jack the Ripper

There is perhaps no more famous serial killer in history than Jack the Ripper, who is made all the more notorious because history isn't quite sure about his identity. Madame Vastra is believed to have killed and consumed him (she found him to be "stringy"), but she could have been mistaken or, more likely, the murders attributed to a single 'Jack the Ripper' were actually performed by multiple people. Officially, Jack the Ripper has never been caught.

Jack is believed to be responsible for at least eleven murders occurring in Whitechapel from 1888 through 1891, although there is some dispute over whether some of the victims were Jack's or simply attributed to him.

Jack is also believed to have written several letters to the police; indeed, the first of these is signed 'Jack the Ripper,' although the handwriting doesn't match other letters and it is believed some, if not all, of them were hoaxes designed to sell newspapers.

Jack the Ripper is an obvious adventure hook for a Paternoster adventure set in 189X. Perhaps Jack is an alien who needs to harvest body parts (like the Clockwork Robots) or simply a deranged serial killer who has been able to elude Scotland Yard. Perhaps alien detectives can succeed where the local authorities have failed?

Unnatural Magic

The Hermetic Order of the Golden Dawn was a magical society created by three members of both the similarly magical Societas Rosicruciana in Anglia and the Freemasons, Samuel Liddell MacGregor Mathers, William Wynn Westscott, and William Robert Woodman. Its core magical teachings are found in the Cipher Manuscripts, notes written on various occult topics, of enigmatic origin (no one knows who wrote them, but likely sometime in the current century).

These writings were 'decoded' over the last two years by Westscott and the Order established its first temple, Isis-Urania, in London this year. Westscott and Mathers also alleged to have contact with a powerful German Rosicrucian, Anna Sprengel, who convinced them to start the order (no hard evidence for Sprengel's existence has ever surfaced and Westcott apparently stopped corresponding with her in 1891). The Golden Dawn also believed in 'Secret Chiefs,' or ascended beings of incredible power, who guided the group from afar.

A similar group that also studies occult practices is the Theosophical Society, which was established in New York City in 1875 and later Madras (Chennai today), India. Unlike the Golden Dawn, the Theosophical Society soon turned to incorporating East Asian religions into their studies and practices. In this year Theosophical founder Helena Blavatsky publishes *The Secret Doctrine* which, like the Golden Dawn, conceives of the idea of 'Hidden Masters,' ascended beings that can teach humanity to become like them.

During these early years of the Golden Dawn, which lasts until Aleister Crowley breaks the silence in 1905, their activities are shrouded in secrecy and divulging any of its activities or secrets is grounds for immediate expulsion. This, coupled with the thrill of learning secret knowledge and belonging to a club that allows women as full members, makes it difficult for members caught performing suspicious activities – such as a man being seen entering a building with a woman other than his wife or a lady in possession of occult texts – to explain themselves. In spite of this – or perhaps even because of this - many celebrities are connected with the Golden Dawn, including authors Alegernon Blackwood, Sir Arthur Conan Doyle, Arthur Machen, Bram Stoker, and W B Yeats.

The Golden Dawn's golden age fits comfortably within 189X and just by reading just the above two paragraphs you should plainly see the potential of using the order, or a close approximate, within a Paternoster campaign. The enigmatic origins of the Order could be framed as alien, whether it be due to an alien mastermind creating an organisation for its own purposes (and perhaps being the inspiration for 'Secret Chiefs') or simply a matter of someone accidentally digging up alien engineering plans and mistaking them for magical geomancy. The Golden Dawn could also be a powerful ally or enemy of the Paternosters, who may even include members within their ranks.

Also, in a world where women are generally seen as second-class citizens, the Golden Dawn offers a plausible reason – if one is needed in a Paternoster campaign – for female characters to be better treated. The Golden Dawn has a relatively vast membership during 189X and it wouldn't be a stretch to 'pepper' members throughout the circles and organisations that the Paternosters regularly interact with – one would likely give great deference to a woman in the outside world if they are comrades in a secret society!

1889 – STRIKES AND SCANDALS

1889 sees developments in several disadvantaged groups, amongst them dock workers. The London Dock Strike raises awareness of the plight of workers and spawned a movement for change, sparking the rise of the Labour Party.

London Dock Strike

One of the big struggles in the industrial revolution is the relationship between employer and employee. Many unskilled labourers flocked to the cities and took jobs on the docks and in factories, only to find low wages, deplorable working conditions and job insecurity. The large gap in bargaining power leads to call for reform and advocates organised strikes and labour unions.

While Britain already has trade unions, new Unions begin to form in this decade to broaden protections to unskilled labourers. The London Dock strike (and, to some extent, the London matchgirls strike the previous year) help to gain public sympathy for the cause, especially since it is non-violent and peacefully resolved. The plight of the working class also fuels several political movements, including anarchism, communism and socialism. Many of these movements organise as the International Workingmen's Association (or First International) in London in 1864. This group soon organises into two camps, with German communist Karl Marx advocating working within government to effect change, and Mikhail Bakunin who calls for more direct action. After many trials and tribulations, a Second International – which excluded the anarchists – is held in Paris this year, calling for an 8-hour work day.

Obviously, the class struggles between the working class and other classes offer adequate fodder for adventure, especially since the authorities are likely to paint all social reformers with the same brush. A peaceful communist could easily be implicated in an anarchist plot that they had nothing to do with. A villain could take advantage of both situations, paying labourers more money for their discretion and aid, and working through socialist parties in order for them to take the fall if things go wrong.

1891 – TECHNOLOGY MARCHES ON

1891 is the last year for Paternoster adventures taking place before the Great Intelligence first attempts to take over the world. Interestingly, given the usual modus operandi for the Great Intelligence's agents (Snowmen and Yeti), the year is marked by a deadly blizzard. On a brighter note (literally!), this is the year that Nicola Tesla introduces the Tesla Coil.

The Blizzard

Southern England is rocked by a blizzard in the second week of March, causing snow to pile up as high as 15-16 feet and is responsible for the deaths of 200 people and 6000 animals, as well as hurricane winds that push ships onto the shore. Much of the region is plunged into chaos as telegraph lines fall and railway lines are covered. At times, thunder and lightning accompany the snowfall.

One of the reasons that the storm catches the population by surprise is that February was unseasonably warm and dry – no one had any reason to suspect a storm. This feels like the basis for a good Paternoster adventure – an alien threat suddenly causes extreme weather and paralyses those caught within it. What makes this storm remarkable is that it is completely natural.

Or was it? The Great Intelligence makes its move to conquer Earth through Walter Simeon the very next year. It's very possible that this blizzard is an early part of that plan, a means through which the Great Intelligence increases its power before creating its Snowmen servants.

Of course, you might also like to use the Blizzard of 1891 as a template for the Blizzard of 189X and could even include the City of London in it this time. Imagine the Seat of Empire paralysed by several feet of snow as an alien invader carries out a nefarious plan. Worse, what happens if the Paternosters are on an excursion at the time the storm hits? Simply getting back into London would be an adventure, made worse by alien agents trying to stop them!

Progress in Leaps and Bounds

While we've quite consciously chosen the nebulous 189X as the setting for **Paternoster Investigations**, we're also aware that there might be some genuine confusion as to how life in 1890s London actually is, compared to popular conceptions of it through Charles Dicken's works and others. It's easy to conflate the 1860s or 1870s with the 1890s and to think of London as a gas-lit city of cobblestone streets, child labourers, hansom carriages and footmen fetching calling cards.

While much of that is still true, London in the 1890s is undergoing many changes that fit more comfortably in the 20th century than the 19th century. Most roads are paved with wooden or granite blocks (although asphalt, once derided as expensive and unsafe for horses, becomes more common to better

HISTORY THROUGH A DIFFERENT LENS

handle motor cars driving over the streets); some are now lit with electric street lights. London also has a telephone system, although regular mail and telegrams are still the dominant means of communication.

Science also continues to fuel the religious debate over evolution, especially with the discovery of the 'Java Man' this year. Its discoverer, Eugene DuBois, publishes his findings in 1894 and posits that Java Man (who we know today as Homo Erectus) is a transitional stage between ape and human. This, of course, fuels much controversy, with some critics claiming that the bones have been misidentified.

189X is an exciting time when new discoveries and inventions are appearing all the time and riling the older generation while being embraced by the new. Some of these discoveries, of course, could be alien in origin, as the Great Intelligence Institute tries to advance human science and the Torchwood Institute collects alien technology. An alien threat might even be surprised by a human invention that it hadn't anticipated when it launched its evil scheme!

1893 – PIERCING THE VEIL

While science marches forward and increasingly reveals the mysteries of nature, there are still those who hold onto older, magical traditions and believe in things that science cannot explain. There are also those who work diligently to debunk these mystical traditions as charlatanry. Others still would take advantage of people who want to believe in something greater, to control and use them, just as Mrs Gillyflower does with her utopian community of Sweetville in this year. Fortunately, the Paternoster Gang, with the Doctor and Clara's help, are able to stop her before she brought a true apocalypse upon the world.

Spiritualism

One of the strongest paranormal concepts in Paternoster London is Spiritism or Spiritualism, which enables communication and interaction between the material world and the invisible world, the latter being inhabited by the spirits of the dead as well as angels and demons (Spiritism believes that human spirits are constantly reincarnated, while Spiritualism accommodates religious beliefs, enabling one to commune with their relatives currently in the afterlife). Spiritualism – we'll use the term generally for both concepts – is frequently paired with Mesmerism during public demonstrations in order to provide wider entertainment for audiences.

In spite of widespread exposure of charlatanry by professed Spiritualists, the movement remains strong throughout the Paternoster era. Grieving mourners find comfort in the possibility of having another opportunity to speak with lost loved ones, and even those who don't believe that contact with the spirit world is possible still find it a useful means of persuading those who do to support various causes.

One interesting by-product of Spiritualism is the Ghost Club, which was founded in London in 1862 and reborn in 1882. The group was created to both investigate allegations of spiritualist activity as well as discuss and possibly contact spirits on their own. This group is active in 189X and continues to this day; notable past members included Charles Babbage and Charles Dickens and current (189X) members include chemist Sir William Crookes and Sir Arthur Conan Doyle. WB Yeats becomes a member early in the next century, but it's little trouble to consider him already a member in 189X.

Spiritualism themes are easy to incorporate into a Paternoster campaign. Aliens such as the Gelth, the Great Intelligence and Sutekh have all used psychic contact to further their agendas. A character who is open to Spiritualism may be more willing to accept the strangeness happening around them when the Paternosters need to draft them to their cause. Even the Paternosters use a variant of this on occasion, contacting each other in a dream state.

Even without the psychic element, spiritualism is a grand illustration of how to dupe people into doing what you want by pretending to provide something in return. It is the promise of a better world and a better life that brings people flocking to Sweetville and, ironically, allows her to work openly in the furtherance of her apocalyptic scheme!

1895 – THE TIME MACHINE

1895 is the default year that we've decided to use for **Paternoster Investigations** whenever we've felt the need to have a more grounded date rather than the nebulous 189X. This is not to say that you are precluded from bringing in events that take place afterwards – far from it! – but given that this year happens a bit after the Doctor's encounters with the Paternoster Gang (thus far) it is a convenient date to use. It also happens to be the year that *The Time Machine* is published!

Inspiring Writers

Given all of the strangeness occurring in Paternoster London it is inevitable that some authors might draw inspiration from such goings on or inventors might mimic what they see in prose. Indeed, the Doctor met a young HG Wells in 1885 and inspired the young man to write several novels based on what he'd encountered over the course of that adventure (see ***Timelash*** in **The Sixth Doctor Sourcebook**). One such book – perhaps his best-known work, *The Time Machine* – is published this year. It can be great fun, especially given the setting, for you to loosely base an adventure on a particular literary work, and then have the characters meet the author of the related work over the course of it!

In fact, the Doctor's meeting with HG Wells is a perfect example of 'massaging' events and timelines in order to make the adventure work. By all accounts, Wells never left southern England, so what was he doing in Loch Ness (he is briefly between jobs, so he's likely on holiday)? He's also dabbling in Spiritualism, learning over the course of his adventure that seemingly magical things are actually the work of science (setting him up for his upcoming novel that pokes fun at Spiritualism, *Love and Mr Lewisham*). For the purposes of the adventure, though, he's simply the appropriate character at the appropriate time interacting with an adventure that inspires his imagination; in a Paternoster adventure, that's all that is required, whether it be HG Wells, Lewis Carroll, Arthur Conan Doyle, Bram Stoker, or even Robert Louis Stevenson (who wrote the *Strange Case of Dr Jekyll and Mr Hyde* in 1886, but dies in 1894).

One thing to keep in mind is that you certainly don't need to limit yourself to late Victorian writers; any early 20th century authors might also fit the bill if they are alive and old enough to remember any strange encounters with the Paternoster Gang in 189X. Algernon Blackwood, Robert Chambers (an American who was studying in Paris until 1893), GK Chesterton, Lord Dunsany, MR James and Arthur Machen all wrote weird tales that could have been inspired by Paternoster adventures. And you don't even need to limit yourself to British authors. If you want to write an adventure that involves lost worlds or Mars, then it's little trouble to say that L Frank Baum or Edgar Rice Burroughs took a holiday in London for a few days in 189X!

1897 – PRETERNATURAL FACT AND FICTION

1897 is notable for two major events in matters esoteric: the announcement that the Satanic Palladian Order was a hoax, and the publication of perhaps the most famous literary horror character of all time, *Dracula*. In an age where science continues to push boundaries, Victorians remain fascinated by the paranormal and much effort is put into exploring, codifying and debunking claims of paranormal activity.

It's important to note that the Victorians' interest in the preternatural or supernatural – or, more generally today, paranormal – didn't begin in the closing years of the Victorian era. Interest in magic and the occult go back centuries and Spiritualism developed in the middle of the century. By the 1880s organisations were springing up to study and debunk paranormal activities.

Debunking Myths

When one watches an illusionist on stage, part of the fun in watching the act is trying to figure out how he is performing his magic. After all, we realise that there is no such thing as real magic, so we understand that the performer's job must be deceiving us in some way. Similarly, in the Victorian era, claims of magical or other paranormal phenomena are met with scepticism and a desire to uncover the 'truth.'

Whole groups, such as the Ghost Club and the Society for Psychical Research (established in 1882), spring up to investigate such claims. The difference between these investigations and stage magic decoding is, of course, that the performers insist that they aren't faking paranormal activity.

Needless to say, most investigations tended to debunk paranormal claims. Across the pond, perhaps the most famous Spiritualist performers, the three Fox Sisters, admit their fraud in 1888 and the contemporaneous Seybert Commission in Pennsylvania has a unanimous record of determining that every case of paranormal activity they investigate to be fraudulent. In 1897 another group turns out to be a hoax: the Palladian Order.

The Palladian Order is the creation of French magazine publisher and writer Leo Taxil, who plays a long game of duping members of the Roman Catholic faith by pretending to have converted to Catholicism while denouncing the 'Satanic' activities (the term 'Satanism' is coined in this era) of a group within the Freemasons, who were dedicated to undermining the Church in order to aid the British Empire. He uses a photograph of one of his typists to portray as the leader, Great Priestess Diana Vaughan, who he also claims was a demon. Taxil manages to keep the subterfuge going until he ends it on his own, pretending that Vaughan is going to appear at a Paris Hall. Taxil then stuns the sold-out audience that the entire Palladian Order is a fraud.

There are two lessons here. The first is that the Doctor's adventures tend to posit that seemingly paranormal – presuming one excludes anything scientific – activities have logical explanations.

The Doctor has encountered two women with psychic abilities that he explained by the fact that they'd lived near temporal rifts, and certain alien rituals, such as those practised by servants of the Daemons and the Fendahl, are simply alien science. Similarly, any alien technology or abilities may be seen as preternatural in origin by Victorian observers.

Secondly, the paranormal has a strong hold on certain people. Even after the Fox Sisters admit their fraud Spiritualism does not end, and the public outing of the Palladian Order does little to dissuade people that Satanic organisations still exist. Indeed, some may say that, given the long periods of time each keeps up the 'ruse,' that something forces them

to pretend it was a hoax all along. Aliens who wish to cloak their activities in mysticism should have no trouble finding locals to dupe.

Count Dracula

Dracula, written by Bram Stoker, is published in 1897. Count Dracula follows in the vein of other literary vampires such as Lord Ruthven, Varney the Vampire and Carmilla. He also follows in the footsteps of other literary characters such as Mr Hyde and the Invisible Man, in that his changed state leads him to do scandalous and evil acts. No doubt the vampire myths are inspired by stories of Saturnynians in disguise (see ***The Vampires of Venice*** in **The Eleventh Doctor Sourcebook**), as well as the Great Vampires that fought the Time Lords and lost (see ***State of Decay*** in **The Fourth Doctor Sourcebook**).

If you are looking for literary inspiration to create peculiar adversaries for the Paternoster Gang then you have a wealth of authors from which to draw upon. Algernon Blackwood and Arthur Machen, both members of the Golden Dawn, write tales about ghosts (possibly references to Gelth or other time-shifted creatures) and the Great God Pan (quite possibly a Daemon given his classical appearance). Lord Dunsany also writes about gods that have a curious resemblance to the Gods of Ragnarok that have faced the Doctor. Robert Chambers, an American author who is still studying in Paris in 189X, pens *The King in Yellow*, referencing both future times, an evil preternatural creature and the mysterious Yellow Sign.

1898 – THE WAR OF THE WORLDS

All good things must come to an end and, presuming you wish for your Paternoster campaign to remain strictly confined to the Victorian era, they must take place before 22nd January 1901, when the Queen dies and her son takes the throne as King Edward VII. One satisfying way to end a Paternoster campaign, or any **Doctor Who Roleplaying Game** campaign, is on an epic note. And, in 1898 HG Wells, inspired by his journey with the Doctor, gave the world *The War of the Worlds.*

A thinly-veiled allegory on imperialism, *The War of the Worlds* posits an alien race, the Martians, who come to Earth to exploit humans and their resources for their own benefit. In spite of their best efforts, mankind is powerless to stop them and it is only an unknown, overlooked weakness – the Martian intolerance of Earthly germs – that destroys them completely.

Sounds familiar, doesn't it?

Substitute in any other alien race and have the Doctor and his companions discover a fatal flaw that, when applied, quickly and completely ends the alien threat and this sounds like a number of the Doctor's adventures. Such a threat, right out of the pages of HG Wells' own novel could provide the Paternoster Gang with a suitably epic finale. An alien force invades London and establishes control. They are seemingly unstoppable until the Paternoster Gang discover its weakness.

Such an adventure would also be an inversion of the imperialist theme, where the imperialists suddenly find themselves in the role of besieged natives. Unlike Wells' Martians, the alien invaders might offer incentives for accepting their rule – better technology, medical miracles or simply the right to live as the aliens take what they want from the planet. The Paternosters might find themselves fighting against the aliens' human allies – perhaps even the Torchwood Institute – as they work to overthrow them.

THE DOCTOR'S VICTORIAN ADVENTURES

There are few better ways to pick up the style and background of the Victorian era than watching the Doctor face an alien menace on the cobbled streets of London. But you will find inspiration not only in the purely Victorian adventures of the Doctor and the Paternoster Gang; the Doctor has visited many worlds that held a certain Victorian aesthetic, even though they were off in the depths of space. Other adventures take their cues from the Gothic horror style so readily associated with the era, even when they too are set on other worlds and in other times.

Let us first take a look at those ***Doctor Who*** episodes set specifically in the Victorian era. Instead of providing these adventures in the order the Doctor experienced them, we'll follow the Doctor as he encountered the age in date order.

THE DOCTOR AND THE AGE

The Doctor has always had a kinship with the Victorian era. From the first moment we saw him he was dressed as a Victorian gentleman. Even in later incarnations, the frock coat has usually been a part of his ensemble. The TARDIS has also had its moments of Victorian charm, from the Fourth Doctor's secondary console room, to the wood and brass fittings of the Eighth Doctor's control chamber and Gothic vaults.

Even as a Time Lord, something about the Doctor has always seemed to have come from Victorian England. He wanders the universe like a Victorian explorer, armed with advanced technology and an unshakable belief in his own superiority. He has the confidence of Victorian privilege, assuming that nothing will have the temerity to offer him harm. But coupled with that is the Victorian wonder at the universe, of unexplored vistas and strange new machines. For all their arrogance, the Victorian English fell in love with the places they conquered. So it should come as no surprise that the Doctor is a frequent visitor, and has a tendency to visit the era (or somewhere a lot like it) at Christmas time.

DARK SHADOWS

The Victorian age is synonymous with Gothic fiction. It is the time of Jack the Ripper, vampires and Frankenstein's monster. Its streets are dark and mysterious, and monsters lurk in their depths. Science is out of control, and madmen fear neither God nor morality in their search for forbidden knowledge. Fantastical tales of horror and mystery found their home in the Victorian age, and many of their tropes remain an essential part of stories set here. Several ***Doctor Who*** adventures take their cues from the Gothic fiction of the Victorian age, without necessarily being set there.

THE DOCTOR'S VICTORIAN ADVENTURES

Gothic Adventures
The Curse of Peladon (Third Doctor)
The Monster of Peladon (Third Doctor)
The Brain of Morbius (Fourth Doctor)
The Stones of Blood (Fourth Doctor)
State of Decay (Fourth Doctor)
Horror of Fang Rock (Fourth Doctor)
Terminus (Fifth Doctor)
The Curse of Fenric (Seventh Doctor)
The Unquiet Dead (Ninth Doctor)
Tooth and Claw (Tenth Doctor)
Ghostlight (Seventh Doctor)
The Talons of Weng-Chiang (Fourth Doctor)
A Good Man Goes to War (Eleventh Doctor)
The Snowmen (Eleventh Doctor)
The Crimson Horror (Eleventh Doctor)
The Name of the Doctor (Eleventh Doctor)
Deep Breath (Twelfth Doctor)

Victorian Adventures
The Next Doctor (Tenth Doctor)
The Evil of the Daleks (Second Doctor)

Victorian Adventures... in Space!
A Christmas Carol (Eleventh Doctor)
The Time of the Doctor (Eleventh Doctor)

The Curse of Peladon: A brooding castle set on a stormy world full of politics and dark deeds. A monster amidst the dark tunnels under the castle, one granted fear and worship in equal measure. The Doctor and Jo Grant had to solve a murder before a delicate political situation stops Peladon joining the galactic federation. See **The Third Doctor Sourcebook**.

The Monster of Peladon: When the Doctor returns to Peladon fifty years later with Sarah Jane Smith, the planet was on the verge of revolt. The Doctor revealed agents were fomenting unrest – a prime theme from the Victorian age – and calmed the situation. See **The Third Doctor Sourcebook**.

The Brain of Morbius: There is no ***Doctor Who*** adventure more worthy of being called 'Gothic' than ***The Brain of Morbius***, for it shares many of the themes with Mary Shelley's classic novel Frankenstein. On the planet of Karn an insane scientist called Solon had preserved the brain of one of Gallifrey's most dangerous criminals, Morbius. When the Doctor arrived, Solon decided his body would be the most appropriate to rehouse his master. This adventure has everything: a stormy planet, a dark castle, a mysterious sisterhood who offer dire warnings, and a mad scientist bent on a dark and terrible plan. See **The Fourth Doctor Sourcebook**.

The Stones of Blood: While this adventure has less of the dark and stormy melodrama of other Gothic stories, there is still a brooding horror to the tale. In this adventure the eponymous stones were an alien lifeform called the Ogri. The Ogri hid in plain sight, but moved about the countryside at night to hunt as they required blood to survive. See **The Fourth Doctor Sourcebook**.

State of Decay: The Fourth Doctor and Romana were lost in E-Space, where they encountered an adventure with parallels to the most famous of Gothic vampire stories. Three ancient undead nobles ruled a land with an iron fist, the peasants working in fear beneath a castle. Once more the dark castle is an important part of the atmosphere, although it turns out to be an ancient spacecraft. Beneath the castle was one of the ancient Great Vampires that the Time Lords fought a terrible war against centuries ago. See **The Fourth Doctor Sourcebook**.

Horror of Fang Rock: When the Fourth Doctor and Leela arrived at Fang Rock, they entered a Gothic tale set on a deserted lighthouse. Here the mysterious horror turned out to be a wounded Rutan killing off the lighthouse inhabitants, but this is easily an adventure the Paternoster Gang might have had in a dark corner of Whitechapel. See **The Fourth Doctor Sourcebook**.

Terminus: The Fifth Doctor found himself in an ancient space station with more in common with a castle or a cavern than a futuristic vessel. It was a dark place, crewed by the desperate and visited by the dying in hope of a cure. The crew wore strange armour and suffered from an illness that made them pale and drawn. It was Nyssa who eventually discovered a potential cure after contracting the virulent 'Lazar's disease' herself. She remained on Terminus to perfect it. See **The Fifth Doctor Sourcebook**.

The Curse of Fenric: The Seventh Doctor and Ace arrived at a quiet village near an army base during the Second World War, where an ancient power began to escape centuries of confinement. These 'vampires' were more monstrous than Gothic, but still appeared out of the mist to claim victims to join their throng. See **The Seventh Doctor Sourcebook**.

ADVENTURES IN THE VICTORIAN AGE

The Next Doctor: Chronologically, the first time the Doctor visited Victorian England was during his tenth incarnation, at Christmas in 1851. Here he met Jackson Lake, a survivor of a Cyberman attack so traumatised that he believed himself to be the Doctor. Together with his companion, Rosita, he teamed up with the Doctor to stop a Cyberman plot to create a huge 'CyberKing' powered by the human mind of Miss Hartigan. The Doctor opened a portal to draw all the Cybermen back into the Void. See **The Tenth Doctor Sourcebook**.

The Evil of the Daleks: The Second Doctor faced his old enemies, the Daleks, when they kidnapped a Victorian scientist in 1867. Professor Waterfield chose to assist the Daleks as they held his daughter Victoria prisoner. The Daleks wanted the Professor to isolate the 'Human Factor' to make more cunning Daleks; however, the plan is also designed to isolate the 'Dalek Factor' which the Daleks intended to infect humanity with. However, the Daleks infected with the 'Human Factor' rebelled. Once more the Daleks were defeated, but the Professor was killed. Victoria joined the Doctor and Jamie on their travels. See **The Second Doctor Sourcebook**.

The Unquiet Dead: The Ninth Doctor accidentally returned to the Victorian age with Rose Tyler in 1869, but landed in Cardiff instead of London. Here, he met Charles Dickens and discovered the dead were being brought back to life by alien creatures made of gas, refugees from the Time War called the Gelth. The Doctor tried to help them, but discovered they were out to conquer a new homeworld. With the help of a psychic housemaid, Gwyneth, the Doctor was able to close the rift the Gelth are using. See **The Ninth Doctor Sourcebook**.

Tooth and Claw: The Doctor first encountered Queen Victoria herself when he and Rose visited Scotland in 1879. Here the sinister Brethren laid a trap for the Queen at the Torchwood Estate, releasing a Werewolf to hunt everyone down. The Doctor saved the Queen, but in doing so proved to Victoria how dangerous and real the threat from aliens was. She ordered the foundation of the Torchwood Institute to study and prepare for such threats, including the Doctor if he should return. See **The Tenth Doctor Sourcebook**.

Ghostlight: The Seventh Doctor arrived with Ace at an old house in 1883. He found that an alien spacecraft had lain beneath the house for hundreds of years. This craft belonged to a being called Light, who was sent to Earth aeons ago to catalogue all its species. He was so distressed to discover everything had changed and his catalogue was out of date he set out to destroy the Earth, but was tricked by the Doctor into destroying himself. See **The Seventh Doctor Sourcebook.**

A Good Man Goes to War: The Eleventh Doctor paid a call on Madame Vastra to collect on her debt. The Doctor summoned many other allies, including Strax, to join his assault on Demon's Run to rescue Amy. After the battle, Vastra and Jenny offered Strax a place to stay with them. It is here that the Paternoster Gang is formed. See **The Eleventh Doctor Sourcebook.**

The Talons of Weng Chiang: The Doctor returned to the streets of Whitechapel in 1892 where a string of murders piques his interest, leading him to a theatre where a famous mesmerist performs. The mesmerist was in league with a time traveller from the future called Magnus Greel, who had become marooned in the age after a failed experiment. But the Doctor tried to convince Greel not to use his time machine again, destroying both it and Magnus Greel when he attempts to use it. See **The Fourth Doctor Sourcebook.**

The Snowmen: Later on, heartbroken at the loss of Amy and Rory to a Weeping Angel, the Doctor retired to 1892 to settle into life as a recluse. The Paternoster Gang did all they could to bring him out of his despair. But it was only when he came across the plans of Dr Simeon and the Great Intelligence that he recovered. Simeon was working with the Great Intelligence to replace humanity with ice creatures under its control. The Paternoster Gang joined the fight, along with a governess called Clara Oswald (whose resemblance to Oswin Oswald intrigued the Doctor, and who later was revealed to be a splinter of the original Clara). Together they broke the Great Intelligence's control over Simeon, and the Great Intelligence lost cohesion. It was scattered and defeated, but not destroyed. See **The Eleventh Doctor Sourcebook**.

The Crimson Horror: In 1893 the Doctor brought the actual Clara to London, much to the surprise of the Paternoster Gang who last saw a splinter of her die. Together they investigated several murders that have left the corpse a bright crimson colour. The trail led them to 'Sweetville', a model town run by Mrs Gillyflower. Mrs Gillyflower and her parasitical alien partner, Mister Sweet, had been preserving those she considered 'perfect' so they might survive an apocalypse she planned to unleash. Those who were not suitable died and turn crimson. The Doctor led the Paternoster Gang to stop Mrs Gillyflower's plans. Mrs Gillyflower and Mister Sweet were both killed as they attempted to launch a rocket to destroy London. See **The Eleventh Doctor Sourcebook**.

The Name of the Doctor: The Paternoster Gang discovered a case they were working on led to the mysterious planet of Trenzalore, where they faced the Great Intelligence once more. He threatened to kill the Paternoster Gang unless the Doctor revealed his name, opening the way to the Doctor's final resting place, an open wound into his own timestream. Clara jumped into the Doctor's timestream to save him and scattered herself across his timeline. She stopped the Great Intelligence from destroying the Doctor. See **The Eleventh Doctor Sourcebook**.

Deep Breath: The Twelfth Doctor arrived in 1894 quite by mistake, soon after his regeneration and with a T-rex in tow. The Paternoster Gang took care of him and Clara as they tried to adjust to his latest incarnation, but they couldn't save the dinosaur, who was killed by Clockwork Robots. The Doctor eventually faced the Half-face Man while the Paternoster Gang and Clara battled his Clockwork Robots. See **The Twelfth Doctor Sourcebook**.

VICTORIAN ADVENTURES... IN SPACE!

Some of the Doctor's adventures are set in places where the tropes, stylings and themes of the Victorian age have been transported to another world.

A Christmas Carol: The spacecraft on which Amy and Rory were enjoying their honeymoon was about to crash on Sardicktown, a planet in the future with a distinctly Victorian feel to it. The ship could only be saved by the strange weather controlling apparatus controlled by Kazran Sardick. But he refused to use it, seeing no purpose or profit in compassion. The Doctor returned to Sardick's childhood and enlisted a beautiful woman called Abigail to inspire empathy in the young man. But Abigail was dying, and as Sardick fell in love with her, this tragedy made him more bitter rather than less. The Doctor helped Sardick finally understand the importance of love and compassion, saving Rory and Amy in the process. See **The Eleventh Doctor Sourcebook**.

The Time of the Doctor: When the Doctor and Clara returned to Trenzalore, they visited the town of Christmas. Ladies walked around in crinoline skirts and children played with hoops and wooden toys. But the Time Lords had opened a crack in space, and called for the Doctor to help them find their way back to this universe. The Doctor's enemies all gathered in orbit to ensure the Time Lords did not return. The Doctor defended the planet for centuries, but as he came to the end of his final regeneration, the Daleks sought to break the siege. But Clara refused to let the Doctor fade away; she used the crack to send a message of her own to the Time Lords. The Time Lords invested him with a new cycle of regenerations and he destroyed the Daleks and saved Christmas. See **The Eleventh Doctor Sourcebook**.

THE PATERNOSTER'S
GUIDE TO LONDON

THE PATERNOSTER'S GUIDE TO LONDON

London is the heart of the United Kingdom and the centre of the British Empire. It has become a crucible for humanity, playing host to people and cultures from across the globe, and even a few from beyond it. Anything and anyone can be found in this vast and rambling city, whether your tastes are for the mysterious, mundane, macabre or even immoral. This great city has grown organically over the centuries, never really been built. It is truer to say the city has been grown, feeding off the souls who have been drawn to it across the ages. Some say that if you listen carefully, in the dead of night, you can hear the city breathe.

For those who are new to the city, London is a maze. The streets are thin and crowded, the buildings crushing together on either side. Roads branch off one another and twist and turn around like veins in the body of the city. Take care not to get lost here; there are dead ends, twisting lanes and shadowed streets that will spin you around if you don't take care. It is as easy to get lost here as it is to lose yourself in the byways and thoroughfares.

As it has grown, London has consumed the small villages that once surrounded it. These villages have become districts, making London a gestalt of many communities rather than a single place. Each area has its own distinct character, sometimes borne of history, other times by immigrant settlers or working communities that have clustered there. The lines between each district are blurred, and only the inhabitants really understand where the boundaries are drawn. The classes gently separate and keep to their own areas of the city, but often the wealthy slide quietly into the seedier places to find illicit entertainment.

DIVIDING THE CITY

While each district of London has its own community and style, most inhabitants break London into five main areas defined by the compass points (North, East, South, West and Central London). However, even these simple divisions often change depending on who you are talking to. There is a lot of area snobbery to contend with too. Those on the borders will often pick which side they would prefer to live on, and get offended if they are included in what they consider to be the less salubrious location. If you asked two people living on the same street which area they lived in, you might get two different answers. As with all things in London, if you live there, you know; anything else marks you as an outsider.

The only natural division in the city is the River Thames, which cuts straight through the middle. It is considered the main dividing line between North and South London, with the centre of Imperial government resting on the north side in the Houses of Parliament. The Thames is the lifeblood of London, and it remains a busy sea port. Vast docks line banks of the river to the East, and provide constant work unloading cargoes from across the empire. Huge sea ships are a constant presence here, but the river is also full of smaller boats using the river to take cargo further inland.

While many areas have a large and particular immigrant population (such as the Chinese community in Limehouse), no area of the city is exclusively the purview of any single group. London is a melting pot where people from many different cultures live side by side. This doesn't mean they mix well, or that there is no bigotry. But it does mean the sight of different or unusual people is not as strange as it might be. Most people are a little more familiar with the various customs and lifestyles of each other's communities. With everyone living so close to each other it is hard to keep too many secrets.

CENTRAL LONDON

Main Districts: The City, Bishopsgate, Covent Garden, Charing Cross

The centre of London is divided between the financial districts and the government buildings that lie among a series of renowned historical sites. While the River Thames runs right through the centre of the city, only the north side is really considered to be Central London. This centre is itself divided into two halves. The eastern half belongs to 'The City' a series of financial institutions that run the economy of both the United Kingdom and the British Empire. These venerable banks and investment companies wield the full mercantile power of Britain, which remains the most powerful weapon in the empire's arsenal. Nations can be swayed by the City with greater ease than using the formidable Royal Navy. The City smells of old money and cold stone.

The western half of the centre is more familiar to tourists and visitors. Here can be found Trafalgar Square, Piccadilly Circus and Leicester Square, around which are a collection of theatres, dance halls and music halls. The most exclusive shops can be found along the triangle of roads formed by Oxford Street, Regent Street, and Tottenham Court Road. Covent Garden plays host to a market bazaar, where plenty of unusual services are available for those who know where to look.

A little further to the west, on the banks of the Thames in Westminster, are the Houses of Parliament. This great Gothic building comprises the House of Lords and the House of Commons, as well as a great clock tower. One of the bells inside (not the tower itself) is famously named 'Big Ben'.

Few people live in Central London. Those who do work in the shops or theatres and live in small tenements crowded above the streets. A few of the wealthy maintain elegant townhouses. But this is mostly so they have a place not too far away when they leave their club.

A BLUFFER'S GUIDE TO PARLIAMENT

Britain and its empire are ruled by a Parliament comprising two separate houses. The House of Commons is made up of the elected representatives of the counties of the United Kingdom. These members are voted for by the residents of their constituency, although not everyone gets a vote. Only adult men of moderate property can vote, which means lower class men, and women of all classes, still have no say.

The House of Lords is an unelected house, whose seats are filled with titled gentlemen. The title passed down through their family carries the right to sit in this house. The Lords cannot make laws in the same way the Commons can, but all new bills must be ratified by the Lords before they can become law.

Two political parties dominate the political landscape, the Conservative (Tory) party and the Liberal Unionist (previously the Whig) party. A new Labour party is gaining growing support among the lower class and is a rising power in politics.

ADVENTURES IN CENTRAL LONDON

The centre of the city is where adventures usually begin and end. It is here you might find a Tyrannosaurus raging by the Houses of Parliament or a mysterious body floating in the river. Usually, the investigation leads you to interview the suspects in their homes outside the centre, or follow a trail to a factory or institution in the suburbs. But when the pieces come together, they often lead back to the centre. Here the characters might chase across the rooftops of Buckingham Palace, dash across Leicester Square or hang from the clock tower of Big Ben.

NOTEWORTHY PLACES IN CENTRAL LONDON

1. Paternoster Row

Next to St Paul's Cathedral is a small street where the Paternoster Gang has made their home. The street got its name from the monks and clergy who would recite the Lord's Prayer (which begins "Pater Noster" in Latin) as they processed along the area. These days the street is much quieter. It lies on the border of the City and very near the new Royal Courts of Justice and several Inns of Court.

This means that many of its residents work in finance or the law and are among the very wealthiest members of society. The area is also close to Fleet Street (the home of most British newspapers) and many booksellers and publishers reside here as well. Its most famous residents are the Paternoster Gang, who have made it known they will consider any case from anyone with the temerity to bring it personally to their door.

2. Covent Garden

This area of London began as a market place, mainly for fruit and vegetables. But as time went on it fell into disrepute. Several taverns, theatres and brothels opened nearby and attracted 'the wrong crowd' in huge numbers. In the late Victorian era the prostitution has moved closer to Piccadilly and the Haymarket, but Covent Garden remains a popular meeting place for the alternative, artistic and bohemian crowds.

The market remains, now a covered building. The surrounding taverns and coffee shops bustle with trade and arguments over art or philosophy spill out onto the pavement. The whole place is loud and often crowded with people of many different classes, with the truly poor selling flowers or matches to the passers-by.

3. The Old Bailey and Newgate Prison

For most of the public, law and order in the city is represented by the bleak shadow of the Old Bailey and its neighbouring building, Newgate Prison. The Old Bailey is a small court for public cases, and given the draconian nature of Victorian law it is not a good place to find oneself. These days most cases are tried in the newly built Royal Courts of Justice, but petty crimes are still heard here and the guilty moved to Newgate next door.

If there is a hell in Victorian England it is Newgate Jail. Even after years of reform it remains a dank stone dungeon, overcrowded with the desperate and the unrepentant. There is little justice here, and the discipline meted out by the guards is brutal. They consider every inmate, be they murderer or pickpocket, to simply be a criminal and treat them the same. For most of the poor, Newgate is a dark embodiment of the injustice of the age.

4. The London Stone
This ancient stone rests in a small nook on Cannon Street in the City of London. It dates back to Roman times and is said to be the founding stone of the city. However, there are tales of it being part of ancient rituals and even worship in days past. For centuries it has survived untouched and watched the city grow around it. This is due in many ways to it being protected by several time travellers.

To navigate space time, unless you have something as advanced as a TARDIS, you need to make use of landmarks. The London Stone is one such landmark, an ancient item present in several time zones at a fixed spatial location (Stonehenge is another, for instance). These landmarks provide time craft with an essential reference point in their travels, so it is in the interests of various time travellers to ensure they remain unmolested. The London Stone's properties might also be useful to those trying to master the secrets of time travel themselves.

The Labyrinth
No one knows where it came from, or who put it there, but under the city is a strange labyrinth of tunnels and corridors. While the only way in is to find an entrance in Central London, it is possible to exit the Labyrinth almost anywhere in the city. Some say the Romans built the city on some form of spatial rift, others that a broken TARDIS lies trapped and dying underneath the streets.

Whatever the truth, the Labyrinth is useful for those who know how to navigate it. Some paths shift and change, but an experienced traveller can find their way. To traverse the Labyrinth you need to look for connections rather than follow the layout. You might follow a trail of numbers etched on the walls, a particular sound or even a feeling. If you follow the corridors themselves, which shift in form and relation from moment to moment, you will surely be lost. Some people have been lost in this maze for years.

TRAP STREET

You might be wondering where to find Trap Street, the alien community Mayor Me runs in 21st century London. In the Victorian age, as you will see on pg. 57, Me is still in the process of building her tiny kingdom.

But that doesn't mean there aren't already other Trap Streets. London is a maze, and many streets are hard to find even when not hidden by alien cloaking technology. There could be all manner of secret nooks just off the main thoroughfare; take care to look for them out of the corner of your eye, but beware what you might find there. Someone willing to hide something so well will rarely be keen to get visitors.

EAST LONDON

Main Districts: Whitechapel, Wapping, Spitalfields, Hackney, Limehouse, Shoreditch

The east side of London is home to its most crushing poverty and most infamous areas. Houses are cheap and crushed together to create rookeries of tight streets and overcrowded communities. Those seeking fame and fortune often find themselves here as their dreams turn to ash. Many criminal gangs make their dens in East London, amidst tangled streets the police will not risk venturing into. Areas like Whitechapel are famous because of the murderers who have haunted the area (such as Jack the Ripper) rather than for their charm or character. But for all this, there is a greater sense of community here. Those who have so little recognise a need to help each other out. Communities pull together, understanding that charity they offer their neighbours will be repaid should they find themselves in need. For this reason the east-enders rarely trust strangers, or the wealthy, but look to their own.

However, that is not to say the wealthy never come here. In fact some of them come here a lot, quietly, at night, to partake in activities they would be ashamed to even mention among their peers. If you know where to look, you can buy anything, or anyone, in the East End. When people have nothing, they will often do anything for the few coins the wealthy have to offer, and so pleasure and degradation come in equal measure in the shadowed streets.

Crime is rife in the area, but usually only among the inhabitants. The wealthy might find their wallet has gone astray at some point in the evening, but they rarely fall victim to violence. It is not in the interests of the local criminals to incite fear in those few who bring money into the area. Better to let them spend it here and then take it from those they give it to. And, if too many wealthy people get hurt, the police take an interest. The establishment cares very little about the lower orders abusing each other, but when a gentleman is assaulted, things are taken more seriously. (It is also important to note that a gentleman's word is never questioned, so if he thinks a certain ragamuffin was responsible, evidence to the contrary is simply rudeness.)

A lot of the work done in the East End revolves around the docks that line the north side of the Thames. The docks here are some of the busiest in the world, and are home to several ship building firms. This is the centre of Britain's mercantile empire and legions of workers swiftly load and unload the ships so more can bring wealth and riches to the capital. While the docks are a place of work, several entertainments surround the place, looking to ensure the workers spend their pay before they get home. Many do just that.

ADVENTURES IN EAST LONDON

The East End is a place of darkness and poverty. Here an investigation will lead to shadowed streets and seedy characters. Nothing will be as it seems and no one will want to reveal their secrets to outsiders. Each clue will peel back another layer, but reveal two more. Then, when the characters get too close to the truth, someone will come to silence them. It might be a knife in the dark or a gang threatening violence in the middle of the street. Out here the law is a distant friend. When the villains are uncovered they will be hard to root out. They can disappear into the maze of lean-to houses, back alleys and quays, to secret lairs well guarded.

NOTEWORTHY PLACES IN EAST LONDON

5. The Murder

One of the most lawless and dangerous places in London is the 'rookery' known colloquially as "the Murder". Here the slum houses are built on top of one another and packed together. People are crushed into homes that form rickety bridges across the wafer thin streets. The area is full of desperate people, rife with thieves, pick pockets and even murderers.

As you might imagine, someone profits from all this, and among the many gangs here, one has risen to prominence in the area. The Murder is ruled by a man known only as 'Johnny Raven' who calls his many followers his 'Crows'. They can be spotted easily as each wears a black feather about their person. Anyone who troubles one of the Crows, or uses a black feather to build their own reputation, is soon found dead. Johnny Raven offers no mercy when it comes to his patch.

6. Limehouse

One of the most renowned districts in London is Limehouse, where the Chinese community has made their home. While the area is not exclusively Chinese, the oriental influence is noticeable in styles of dress and decoration. When you enter the district, there is sometimes a sense of stepping into another world, and it is an atmosphere the residents encourage. Several gangs of Tongs and Triads have made their home here too, and so even the criminal element remains a little different from the rest of London.

Limehouse is known for its Opium Dens, small smoky places where clients can lose themselves to the euphoria of the opium pipe. The practice is not illegal (in fact, Britain fought two wars to force China to continue trading opium with them) but it is considered deeply unseemly. As usual, the Chinese community is blamed for 'peddling this filth' rather than the clients admonished for seeking it out.

7. The Ten Bells
One of the most well known pubs in the East End is the Ten Bells, which sits on the 'nicer' edge of Whitechapel. It serves as a community centre for the area and has become the best place to pick up the local gossip. It also forms the 'business offices' of several rather shady characters who might be engaged for (or require) a myriad different services.

What makes the Ten Bells especially interesting is that it also caters for several wealthier clients. While there is a clear divide between the more sedate Saloon Bar and the Public Bar, customers come here from all walks of life. The beer is cheap enough for the lower class to afford it, but good enough for the wealthy to risk drinking it. The middle class are as common here as the lower class when both the offices and docks close for the day and the workers need a bite to eat. As night falls, wealthy gentlemen looking to make a foray into the darker delights of the East End stop here for a few ales to give them a spot of Dutch courage. In short, you might meet anyone if you enter the Ten Bells. The pub is owned by Josiah and Penny Spent, and their two teenage daughters (Sarah and Mary) often wait on the tables. They are an ordinary upper lower class family as far as most people are concerned. But in fact they are time travellers from the 52nd century, part of a community who believe it is spiritually better to live in a simpler time. This usually means they all know a lot more than people expect them to know, and they listen to the comings and goings of their clientèle with great interest.

8. Loin Street
Not far from Smithfields meat market, is another form of market that caters to more specialised customers. The Loin Street market is a collection of small stalls that sell various cuts of meat, not all of which is animal. The various meat suppliers source and supply meats from all manner of places off-world for those with a more 'specific' palette. While the market insists it has strict rules about meat taken from sentient species, this policy is barely policed. Alien residents who don't have the time to hunt the streets of London can often find something suitable for dinner, if they talk to the right person.

9. The Palace Theatre
This small theatre lies close by to Limehouse, but still has pretensions of being in the West End. Managed by Henry Jago, the Palace plays host to a turbulent variety of acts. The line up is rarely the same two nights running, although if Jago has a good money spinner you can be assured of seeing it every night until he has thoroughly rung every coin from it. As well as running the theatre, Jago also serves as a master of ceremonies and the theatre has a loyal but hard to please audience. Beneath the theatre is an access panel to a lair formerly occupied by Magnus Greel (see page 32). This lair links into the sewers and might make a useful getaway tunnel, if you can get past his giant rats.

WEST LONDON

Main Districts: Belgravia, Pimlico, Kensington & Chelsea, Mayfair

The most salubrious area of London is the West End, where the wealthy promenade in its glorious parks or dine in its expensive clubs. In stark contrast to the East End, West London has the most expensive real estate and the most spacious streets and houses in the city. Three of London's great parks are found here (Regent's Park, St James's Park and Hyde Park), which play host to open air music and a vibrant social scene. On sunny days these parks fill with the wealthy, either walking together or trotting along in open carriages, where they exchange news and gossip with their peers. The smog and shadow of the city is absent here, and the poverty of the lower classes easily ignored.

ADVENTURES IN WEST LONDON

In the West End, evil dresses very well indeed. To investigate here the characters had better behave properly or doors will politely but firmly shut in their faces. The villains of the West End are among the most privileged families, and may see their crimes as nothing more than taking what is theirs by right. They will certainly find any characters with the temerity to question their actions to be rude and insulting. In the West End, the police will be of little help. While they can be easily found, they will not want to arrest anyone as well connected as the people who live here. Even the police won't question the word of a gentleman; even one found standing over a body with a knife in his hand.

However, the West End is not populated entirely with villains. Even the wealthy and privileged find themselves victims of crime, now and again. Sometimes this will have the potential to provoke a scandal – something the wealthy tend to avoid. When it comes to investigating such crimes, the wronged party may well seek out the characters for their discretion rather than turning to the police. If they do not tread carefully in their investigation, the scandal may prove worse for their client than the original crime.

NOTEWORTHY PLACES IN WEST LONDON

10. The Andromeda Club

Nestled in the 'clubbable' area of Pimlico is one of the most exclusive clubs in London. However, the Andromeda Club works very hard to ensure no one notices quite how exclusive it actually is. This is because membership in the club is only available to non-humans, and the members themselves do not want this fact widely known. The Andromeda Club is designed for wealthy aliens who usually hide their existence behind a carefully managed façade. Everyone who passes through the doors of the club appears human. But once inside they remove their masks, skin suits, shimmers, make up and veils, able to finally relax.

Membership is exclusively by recommendation from another member. However, the only real qualifications required are that the new member be an alien and be able to pay the expensive monthly fees. In return for these fees each member has the full run of the extensive club building and its facilities. These include all manner of special resources for aliens, such as mud baths for scaly skin, an extensive menu of non-terrestrial foods, different atmospherically controlled club rooms and newspapers and journals from all over the galaxy. Essentially the club can duplicate any form of environment for the comfort of its members and provide a connection to news from the rest of the universe.

As humans are not allowed to even enter the club, Jenny has never been but Madame Vastra is a member. Vastra did give Strax membership as a birthday present once. However, the club's insistence that weapons being left with the concierge rather put him off.

11. The Adventurer's Society

This club for explorers was founded just five years ago, rather controversially by a lady explorer called Eloise de Winter. The heir to a vast fortune, Lady de Winter had already caused a stir in society by using her wealth to fund several expeditions. Her relatives were highly concerned that if her wealth was frittered away on such rash things she might never secure an offer of marriage. However, Eloise was more than content to remain single and use her funds as she pleased.

Now aged 65, Eloise finally decided she wasn't well enough to travel as much as she would like. But she still longed to hear of the exploits of other adventurers and explorers, so she founded a club for

travellers in the heart of Mayfair. The Adventurer's Society is open to all, no matter their class, so long as they have travelled to foreign shores. Entrance is a simple affair. An applicant must entertain the committee over dinner with tales of their adventures. If they prove entertaining, and can afford the modest fees, they will be granted admission.

The society functions mainly as any other club, but, as a gathering of explorers, it also provides several other benefits. Firstly, the society offers the collective experience of its members. There is no shortage of people to ask about almost any area of the globe and how to find your way there.

An evening soliciting advice over drinks with the membership before an expedition might literally save lives. There are also many potential expedition partners among the assembly, so most members look for travelling companions here as well. Merchants who sell expedition supplies clamour to become 'recognised' by the society, which guarantees a brisk trade and marks their goods as both reliable and tested in the field.

SOUTH LONDON

Main Districts: Battersea, Lambeth, Rotherhithe, Greenwich, Southwark

South London is a place of steam and sweat. Found here is a mixture of factories and developing housing. If the middle class have a part of the city, it is here, where they can be close to the factories and industries they run. Along the riverbank are an array of warehouses, factories and production facilities that power the city's manufacturing base. But further south from the smoke and grime the middle class are laying claim to their own part of the city.

New housing developments, too expensive for the poor and not salubrious enough for the upper classes are attracting the wealthy middle class. Here they are looking to craft a new domain, one from where they can take power from the wealthy.

ADVENTURES IN SOUTH LONDON

South London is a place of dichotomy and division. Near the river are the factories, pumping out heat and smoke. But as you move further south the city becomes green with parkland and expensive new homes. South London switches between the compressed and oppressive production facilities and the homes of the nouveau riche. It has its own community, divided into the workers and the factory owners.

The upper classes find it gauche and the poor lower class can't afford to be there. Investigations will find the middle classes close ranks very quickly. Workers will say nothing for fear of losing their jobs, and the wealthy will keep their secrets to maintain the growing reputation of the area. Something is coming to the boil here.

NOTEWORTHY PLACES IN SOUTH LONDON

12. Royal Observatory, Greenwich
Since 1675 the observatory at Greenwich has been the premier astronomical research centre of Britain. It nestles amidst gentle parkland atop a tall hill. It has been a place for both serious academics and gentleman scholars for many years. Most famously it is also home to the Meridian line, the point from which Longitude and time are measured across the world.

In addition to its astronomical work, the observatory also plays host to a secretive group of Torchwood agents. Codename: Vigilate Caelum (or "Skywatch"), the group are responsible for watching the night sky to guard against alien invasion. Several royal charters give the group the right to use the telescopes as and when they want, which ruffles the feathers of most other academics. The Torchwood agents here are highly secretive, especially about the extra devices they often attach to their equipment. They are the vanguard of Earth's defence, logging and reporting any strange activity they see in the night sky. But even with the more advanced technology they have at their disposal, the odd alien craft does get past.

13. The Ale Society
This small but growing group meets in the Wheatsheaf Pub near Kennington Park, and has done so since the 1850s. As far as anyone knows, the group are a working class social club who hire the back room of the pub out to sample new ales. However, the society is more than it seems, and it is no coincidence they meet overlooking the park where many Chartist meetings have gathered before.

The Ale Society is actually a gathering of the leaders of several anarchist and chartist cells across London. In 1848, the movement gathered a huge demonstration that so frightened the establishment there were nearly as many police as there were demonstrators. The Ale Society has not forgotten and continues to meet and recruit in the hopes of making a more noteworthy form of civil resistance.

Most of the members of the Ale Society are peaceful men and women looking for social change and equality for the poor. However, over the last few years, the hardliners have grown in power within the society. They believe peaceful demonstration and lobbying are doomed to failure. They seek to convince the society to move towards a more aggressive policy and include acts of vandalism and terrorism. So far the society has resisted this change, but it will not be long before someone decides to take matters into their own hands.

14. The Bethlehem Royal Hospital
The current incarnation of the infamous 'Bedlam' hospital resides in Southwark. This building is the third to bear the name; it was previously in Bishopsgate and Moorfields and there are plans to rebuild it once more soon in West Wickham. Since 1247 it has been an institution for the care of the insane. But, given the standards of psychiatric care it has always been more of a place to keep the mad locked up rather than as a centre for healing and therapy. Its nickname of 'Bedlam' has become synonymous with chaos, noise and terror.

While it is not a place many visit out of choice, some of its inmates possess valuable information. Those who insist they have seen aliens or spacecraft will find themselves here. The same is also true of those who fall victim to certain species that prey on the mind. Many people enter the walls of Bedlam perfectly sane but misunderstood, and it is the place itself that drives them mad.

NORTH LONDON

Main Districts: Hampstead, Camden, Highgate, Islington

Out beyond the glamour of Central London, North London is a more pastoral part of the city. Here the creeping brickwork is gradually enveloping outlying villages. But many still maintain their character and village lifestyle. While they are firmly part of the city, the districts of North London still remember when they were small villages. The more parochial attitudes persist, and among the brick tenements, old traditions remain.

Communities here tend to think of themselves as slightly outside the city. Their loyalty is to the village they still see here, not the city that has overlaid it. The individual communities keep to themselves and consider even those from the neighbouring district as outsiders.

There is a good mixture of residents here, although most are upper lower class or lower middle class. The area is not fashionable enough for the wealthy upper class, or 'up and coming' enough for the rising entrepreneurs of the upper middle class, so it remains a place of craftsmen and shop keepers. The many markets here bustle with local trade goods and many gems can be found if you know where to look.

ADVENTURES IN NORTH LONDON

Investigations here will be quite difficult if the characters are 'outsiders'. They will find plenty of doors closed to them, albeit with a polite smile. North London is a place of secrets that everyone knows but no one will tell. Most people know each other's business, but they won't share it with people they don't know. The residents do not want the city coming right up to their door and spoiling the status quo here.

North London is quiet and spacious, with plenty of open commons and wide streets. There are few places to hide, unless you know someone who can hide you. Running and shouting will not be tolerated and what might barely turn a head in the city will deeply shock the less 'modern' North Londoner.

NOTEWORTHY PLACES IN NORTH LONDON

15. The TARDIS Cargo Delivery Company

Many years ago, a man named Jackson Lake used to own a balloon he referred to as his TARDIS (Tethered Aerial Release, Developed In Style). He never actually flew it, instead leaving it in the care of a man called Jed. Jed knew quite a lot about balloons and ballooning in general and believed that this form of air travel might have a future.

After the defeat of the CyberKing, Jackson Lake had little use for his TARDIS, and so granted it to Jed for his loyal service. Seeing an opportunity, Jed began a small business offering aerial views of the city for a modest fee. The tours proved popular, and Jed was able to employ more pilots and buy more balloons. He began to invest in new technology, and it wasn't long before the company acquired its first airship and begun doing commercial deliveries.

Jed eventually retired, leaving the business in the hands of his children Henry and Charlotte. They moved the business to North London and now own three airships, which can be hired for private trips or to carry cargo across the country. The original TARDIS remains in their care, floating over the main hangars as the symbol of the business.

16. The Undercourt

In a small house in Camden, a group of lawyers and judges meet in secret to hear unusual cases that would cause scandal and shock were they to be reported in the press. For this court is there to settle disputes between the many aliens that live in secret in the capital. If both parties agree, the court will hear

their case and pronounce judgement, a judgement that is binding for both parties. The court is made up of three judges at any one time. Their decision on any matter is considered final.

The court was created to maintain the anonymity of the members of London's alien community and settle disputes without involving human authorities. Few amongst the community want to answer the awkward questions that might result from their unusual nature, so the court settles matters before they get to the attention of the police. While it follows English law it does take into account the sensibilities and customs of alien cultures too.

The Paternoster Gang have been hired on a few occasions to bring accused before the court. Some, especially the guilty, would rather make a run for it when called to give evidence. However, Madame Vastra has refused to act as an executioner (as the court can impose a death sentence), maintaining a rather cynical opinion of the court's motives.

17. Highgate Cemetery

In 1832 seven new cemeteries were built around London to cope with the vast amount of burial space required by the expanding population. Before this time bodies were buried on top of one another in stacks sometimes twenty deep. Even this new development was unable to cope with demand, leading to the opening of Brookwood Cemetery in 1849. Brookwood was the largest cemetery at the time, and a special train from Waterloo took both the living and the dead (charging a return or single ticket as appropriate) to what became known as the 'London Necropolis'.

Highgate Cemetery is the best known of the seven new cemeteries, perhaps one of the most mysterious burial grounds in the city too. It has several famous residents interred within its gently wooded grounds. Two avenues of tombs create strange streets between the grave sites, where angels weep for the dead.

Highgate is a place of mysteries. Many people have used the graves and tombs to hide objects and people from prying eyes. Secrets are buried here along with the dead. The peace of the place is distracting and it is easy for the unwary to get lost among the stones. Amongst all of this, the angels preside, watching from the graves of the famous and the forgotten. People have been known to go missing when they walk alone, day and night. Only the statues might tell you their fate, but so many of them cover their faces and look away.

PATERNOSTER IRREGULARS

In addition to the full members of the Paternoster Gang, there are a number of 'Irregulars,' 'civilians' upon whom the Paternosters call when they have specific needs. Some Irregulars could be considered allies or even friends; others offer their services only grudgingly.

Each Irregular has 2 Story Points – this is because an Irregular is only intended to be called upon once or twice during an adventure. If you plan to have an Irregular play a larger role in a particular adventure then you may wish to increase this number.

PROFESSOR AUGUSTA BARLOW

Augusta Barlow is a brilliant engineer and scientist who teaches as a professor at Cambridge. Her father was an engineer and was trying to develop a better 'steam carriage', when both he and her mother succumbed to the choking conditions of the London pea-souper. Driven by this tragedy, Augusta turned her attention away from coal-burning steam and considered electricity to be the fuel of the future, hoping to create a smokeless London.

Initially rebuffed by the scientific community, Augusta had inherited enough of a fortune to continue her work in private. She'd gained some unorthodox (and society-damaging) allies in the process, eventually drawing the attention of the Torchwood Institute, who decided that giving Augusta alien artefacts to analyse would provide plausible deniability if anything bad happened.

As it turned out, Augusta became a valued resource and although she rejected formal recruitment she offered to remain a consultant if the Torchwood Institute could remove the barriers keeping her from becoming a professor.

Today, Augusta enjoys her work, finding working with questioning students exciting and essential to challenging her theories and giving her inspiration. Her mind is 10-20 years ahead of her time and she drives an electric car, leading to her school nickname of 'Professor Lightning.' She has crossed paths with Madame Vastra on several occasions and she's perfectly happy to help the Paternoster Gang as much as she does Torchwood.

PROFESSOR LIGHTNING

AWARENESS	3	PRESENCE	4
COORDINATION	3	RESOLVE	4
INGENUITY	5	STRENGTH	2

SKILLS
Convince 2, Craft 5, Knowledge 4, Medicine 2, Science 4, Technology 5, Transport 5.

TRAITS
Boffin: Augusta can create Gadgets, especially those that utilise electricity as the power source.
Eccentric (Minor): Augusta lives in an electrical world; her home is powered by it and she often displays its effects. While electricity is certainly gaining acceptance, it is still unusual enough to make her seem eccentric to her peers and students. She also tends to wear goggles rather than spectacles, furthering her eccentricity.
Friends (Major): Augusta has both the resources of a major university as well as the Torchwood Institute at her disposal.
Impaired Senses (Minor): Augusta wears spectacles (well, goggles). Without them, she suffers a -2 penalty to rolls relying on sight.
Insatiable Curiosity: Augusta is curious and will investigate anything that sparks her curiosity unless she passes a Resolve + Ingenuity roll at -2.
Obsession (Minor): Augusta is committed to a cleaner London and pursues any scientific advance towards that goal.
Resourceful Pockets: Augusta tends to have bits of useful stuff on her person. Roll two dice and get a 'double' (or spend a Story Point) if she needs something.
Technically Adept: Augusta gets a +2 to any Technology roll to fix a broken or faulty device.
Time Traveller: While technically not a time traveller, Augusta's keen mind and analysis of alien artefacts enables her to grasp items from futuristic civilisations. She can understand items from TL 7 and lower.

TECH LEVEL: 4 STORY POINTS: 2

NURSE JANET BLACKWOOD

Janet Blackwood is a nurse at Bedlam Hospital, but she also volunteers her services in various clinics throughout the city. Born into poverty, Janet initially made her living on the street corners of Whitechapel until she was 'discovered' by a theatre owner and became an actor. While her acting skills were mediocre at best – and the less one says about her singing voice the better – Janet's striking appearance garnered many admirers and she supplemented her income by continuing to practice her old profession amongst the wealthier theatre patrons.

Janet's acting and prostitution careers both came crashing to an end when one of her clients turned out to be a serial killer. Fortunately, Madame Vastra was tracking the killer and stopped him – not to mention making an exquisite meal out of him – before he was able to kill her. In return for Janet's discretion, Vastra offered her a chance at a new life and secured an education for her as a nurse as well as an eventual position at the Royal Bethlehem Hospital. As part of the agreement, Janet informs the Paternoster Gang of any particularly strange patients or occurrences at Bedlam or the clinics that she helps throughout the city. In addition, she can lean on former clients to extract favours or information, although she loathes to do this, not the least because there have been at least two attempts on her life by hired thugs looking to ensure her silence.

NURSE BLACKWOOD

AWARENESS	3	PRESENCE	3
COORDINATION	4	RESOLVE	3
INGENUITY	2	STRENGTH	2

SKILLS
Athletics 2, Convince 3, Fighting 2, Medicine 4, Subterfuge 3, Survival 3.

TRAITS
Adversary (Minor): There are a few 'previous acquaintances' of Janet who believe that doing away with her would better keep their secrets.
Attractive: Janet is a very attractive woman and gets a +2 bonus on any rolls that involve her looks.
Empathic: Janet is good at reading people, receiving a +2 bonus to do so.
Obligation (Minor): Janet works odd hours at the hospital and can always be called in.
Owed Favour (Minor): Janet has had past dalliances with people who'd otherwise like to forget. Occasionally she can get information from them in return for her continued silence.
Run for Your Life! Janet gets a +1 bonus to her speed when evading pursuit.
Unadventurous: Janet just wants a quiet life.

TECH LEVEL: 4 STORY POINTS: 2

PATERNOSTER IRREGULARS

LORD ALEXANDER FITZSTEPHEN

Whenever Madame Vastra needs highly placed protection she calls upon Lord Alexander Fitzstephen, the Earl of Shaftfield. With his prestige and seat in the House of Lords, Alexander can make most problems disappear. Ironically, this power so often appreciated by the Paternoster Gang is wielded by a timid man who avoids scandal at any cost.

LORD ALEXANDER

AWARENESS	3	PRESENCE	2
COORDINATION	3	RESOLVE	2
INGENUITY	3	STRENGTH	2

SKILLS

Athletics 1, Convince 4, Knowledge 3, Marksman 2.

TRAITS

Cowardly: Alexander suffers a -2 penalty on any roll when he needs to resist running away screaming.

Dark Secret (Minor): While Alexander has endured possible scandal by publicly accepting Gabrielle as his daughter, he fears the scandals that will arise should her illicit activities become known.

Friends (Major): As a member of the House of Lords, Alexander has many friends upon whom he can call for aid.

Noble: Alexander is an Earl, which gives him a +2 bonus in social situations against those of lesser title or common.

Owed Favour (Minor): Alexander has helped enough people in small ways that he can call upon them for minor assistance.

TECH LEVEL: 4 STORY POINTS: 2

Lord Alexander was a disappointment to his father and previous Earl, Lord Henry. In his father's eyes Alexander's 'effeminate' mannerisms and 'spineless' personality encouraged Henry to be especially hard on his son. With his older brother William held up as a role model, Alexander followed him into the military. The Earl's influence ensured Alexander a good posting in Calcutta, where he fell in love with a local woman and had a child with her.

Unfortunately, Alexander's older brother William died in the Zulu War and, as the heir, the Earl, now in declining health, ordered him home. Fearing his father's wrath Alexander left his wife and child behind, rationalising that he'd bring them to England after his father's death. His father, however, lingered for several years. By the time the Earl died Alexander had grown accustomed to this arrangement and even remarried at his father's behest, sending his first wife divorce papers via post.

Everything changed for Lord Alexander when his daughter arrived in London, bringing news that her mother had died and that she wanted to see her father again. Fearful of scandal, Alexander tried to placate her with money, but Gabrielle Fitzstephen refused to take it. Ironically it was Lord Alexander's second wife, Beatrice, who accepted Gabrielle and Lord Alexander allowed her to stay with them.

Gabrielle proved something of a nuisance, however, when her anarchist tendencies and thieving ways netted her a strange artefact from an antiquities dealer.

This artefact turned out to be a Krynoid pod, which infested the gardens of the Shaftfield estate and would have killed Lord Alexander were it not for the timely intervention of Madame Vastra and the Doctor. Extremely grateful for their assistance, Lord Alexander pledged to help Vastra in any way he can, so long as she can help keep his wayward daughter's activities out of the headlines.

GABRIELLE FITZSTEPHEN

Gabrielle Fitzstephen is an upper-class burglar who is something of a Robin Hood; she robs from the rich and gives most of what she acquires to the poor.

She is also a major thorn in the side of her father, Lord Alexander Fitzstephen, who does his best to cover her crimes in order to stave off scandal. This includes securing the services of the Paternoster

Gang to 'clean up' after Gabrielle. Needless to say, this does not endear the thief to Madame Vastra, who feels that her time is better spent on 'legitimate cases' rather than dealing with what is ultimately a domestic issue between father and daughter.

Gabrielle is considered a 'Eurasian' (born of English and Indian parents) and was born when her father was stationed in Calcutta during his time as a servant for the British Raj. She remained behind with her mother when he returned home, her mother having accepted a divorce in return for an annual stipend. When her mother died, Gabrielle decided to come to Great Britain to be with her father.

GABRIELLE FITZSTEPHEN

AWARENESS	4	PRESENCE	4
COORDINATION	5	RESOLVE	5
INGENUITY	6	STRENGTH	3

SKILLS
Athletics 3, Convince 4 (Fast Talk 6), Craft 3, Fighting 4, Knowledge 3, Marksman 3, Subterfuge 4 (Lockpicking 6), Survival 3, Transport 2.

TRAITS
Argumentative: Gabrielle will argue her point of view even if it puts her life in danger.
Attractive: Gabrielle gets a +2 bonus to any rolls that involve her looks.
Distinctive: Gabrielle's Indian heritage gives her a -2 penalty to rolls to blend into London society. Others have a +2 bonus to remember or recognise her.
Hot Shot: Gabrielle is used to commandeering hansoms and coaches to facilitate her escapes. She gets a +2 bonus to Transport rolls.
Keen Senses (Major): Gabrielle gets a +2 to all Awareness rolls.
Lucky: Gabrielle may re-roll any 'double 1s'.
Obsession (Minor): Gabrielle is consumed with her fight for social justice.
Outsider: As a foreigner, Gabrielle is treated differently and gets a -2 on social rolls with strangers.
Quick Reflexes: Always goes first in a round.
Run for Your Life! Gabrielle gets a +1 bonus to her speed when fleeing.
Sense of Direction: +2 bonus to any navigation roll.

TECH LEVEL: 4 STORY POINTS: 6

ADA GILLYFLOWER

Ada Gillyflower is the daughter of Mrs Winifred Gillyflower, a power-mad woman under the influence of an alien parasite who sought to purify the world by wiping out all but a select few. In order to perfect her process, Mrs Gillyflower secretly experimented on her own daughter, which left Ada blinded and covered in red blemishes all over her body. The Paternoster Gang, with help from the Doctor and Clara, prevented the plan. Mrs Gillyflower fell to her death and Ada crushed the alien parasite.

Madame Vastra helped Ada resettle in London, where the young woman was determined to make her own way, having given away most of her family fortune to help those whom her mother harmed. She found that her blindness was not a large impediment to being a telegraph operator, as she easily memorised Morse code and the letter keys on a keyboard. She enjoys working long hours and spends much of her time chatting with other telegraph operators. This, coupled with the information gleaned from sending and receiving telegrams, has made her a valuable resource when the Paternosters need to gather intelligence. Ada is only too grateful to help.

Outside of her work, Ada has two constant companions. The first is her guide dog K-9, a gift given to her as a housewarming gift by the Doctor, whom she affectionately refers to as her 'monster.' Unlike other versions of K-9 this one is simply a highly trained flesh-and-blood golden retriever, albeit a slightly telepathic one from the 23rd century. The other is Mr Edmund Higgins, a co-worker who is positively smitten with Ada.

ADA GILLYFLOWER

AWARENESS	2	PRESENCE	3
COORDINATION	2	RESOLVE	2
INGENUITY	3	STRENGTH	5

SKILLS

Athletics 2, Convince 3, Fighting 2, Knowledge 2, Survival 3, Technology 3 (Telegraph 5).

TRAITS

Animal Friendship (Minor): Exposure to K-9 has given Ada a special connection with other animals as well, and she can do things like sit on a horse and have it take her where she needs to go, or calm down guard dogs that might otherwise attack her.

Brave: Ada gains a +2 bonus to any Resolve roll when she needs to show courage.

Distinctive (Minor): Due to the scars on her face, Ada takes a -2 penalty to rolls to blend in. Others have a +2 bonus to remember or recognise her.

Impaired Senses (Major): Ada is blind, although she can 'see' through the eyes of K-9.

Keen Senses (Minor): Given her profession and her need to compensate for lack of sight, Ada has learned to rely on her hearing and gains a +2 to Awareness rolls involving hearing.

Percussive Maintenance: Ada may reroll failed attempt to use technology – especially telegraphy equipment – after striking it (only one reroll allowed). She may also temporarily 'repair' broken technology this way.

Special – Slightly Telepathic: Ada is psychically connected to K-9 and can share her desires and commands without speaking to him. This same connection can be used on other animals as well, but it usually requires a Presence + Convince roll to get animals to act as she wishes.

TECH LEVEL: 4 STORY POINTS: 2

INSPECTOR TOBIAS GREGSON

Inspector Tobias Gregson is a capable Scotland Yard detective who isn't afraid to put success before pride in order to solve a case.

He genuinely values the assistance of consulting detectives, no matter how unorthodox their appearance or methods, and this has brought him to seek Madame Vastra's assistance on several cases when peculiar circumstances are involved.

Given the barbs and teasing that he's willing to take from Madame Vastra and the Paternoster Gang, Gregson is sometimes seen as timid. This, however, is a mistake, as Gregson fully asserts himself when necessary. He simply understands that the results he gets from the Paternosters are worth the occasional joke at his expense.

Gregson is usually the catalyst of a Paternoster investigation, calling upon them when something seems peculiar in a particular case. It's his detective's badge that often gets the Paternoster Gang access and information where they may otherwise find difficulty.

INSPECTOR TOBIAS GREGSON

AWARENESS	4	PRESENCE	4
COORDINATION	3	RESOLVE	4
INGENUITY	3	STRENGTH	2

SKILLS

Athletics 2, Convince 3, Fighting 2, Knowledge 3, Marksman 3, Subterfuge 2.

TRAITS

Brave: He gets a +2 bonus on Resolve rolls when he could get scared or needs to show courage.

Friends (Major): As a detective for the Metropolitan Police, Gregson has many official friends he can go to for aid – as well as a few 'unofficial' ones.

Obligation (Major): Gregson sometimes works long hours on a case.

Voice of Authority: Gregson gets a +2 bonus to Presence and Convince rolls

TECH LEVEL: 4 STORY POINTS: 2

MADAME ESTHER HOROWITZ

A short, stocky, middle-aged woman with a thick Eastern European accent, Madame Horowitz runs an apothecary in Islington. She is also a powerful psychic, having been born near a temporal rift in the Bohemian countryside. She immigrated with her parents when she was young and is now a respected member of the community. She runs a small tea and pastry shop, although those in the know seek out her more esoteric services – as a fortune teller.

MADAME HOROWITZ

AWARENESS	4	PRESENCE	4
COORDINATION	3	RESOLVE	5
INGENUITY	2	STRENGTH	2

SKILLS
Craft 5 (Baker 7), Knowledge 2, Medicine 2, Survival 2.

TRAITS
Distinctive: Esther's strong personality and thick accent ensures that she stands out in a crowd.
Feel the Turn of the Universe: Esther is one of those rare humans who can sense that something is wrong in the universe, if she first makes an Awareness + Ingenuity roll with a +2 bonus.
Precognition: By spending a Story Point, Esther can see the future of anyone whose presence she is in.
Psychic
Psychic Training: Esther can block her mind from intrusion, getting a +2 bonus to Resolve rolls.
Unadventurous: Esther is happy in her new home and is loath to leave it. For someone with such an open mind she has no wish to travel or get involved in Paternoster investigations.

TECH LEVEL: 4 STORY POINTS: 2

Madame Horowitz came to the attention of the Paternoster Gang when investigations in Islington kept turning up mention of her name. It was Jenny Flint who first had her fortune told by Madame Horowitz, where she discovered that her visions were quite specific and unerringly accurate; since then the Paternosters have engaged her services whenever they're stuck on a particularly difficult case.

Madame Horowitz's visions are best when she has the subject in front of her, so Jenny often bring suspects or victims to her in order to get psychic impressions. Madame Horowitz is only too glad to help and sometimes calls upon Jenny to return the favour whenever she feels an extremely strong premonition or when someone in her community is in trouble. In addition to being a strong psychic, Madame Horowitz's strudel is second to none.

KARRATUDDORANNA

Karratuddoranna is a Zocci criminal who was exiled to Earth. Trying to blend in, Karratuddoranna uses mascara to change the hue of her face and grinds down her facial spikes to make them appear to be moles. She has adopted the name 'Karen,' but Jenny's nickname for her, 'Freckles' has stuck.

FRECKLES

AWARENESS	3	PRESENCE	4
COORDINATION	5	RESOLVE	3
INGENUITY	3	STRENGTH	1

SKILLS
Athletics 3, Convince 3, Fighting 1, Knowledge 3 (London Underworld 5), Subterfuge 4, Survival 3.

TRAITS
Alien
Alien Appearance: While Freckles disguises her face, the rest of her body, including the top and back of her head, remain alien in appearance (she usually wears a hat or wrap).
Cowardly: Freckles prefers discretion to valour.
Face in the Crowd: Freckles is very adept at looking innocent and unassuming. She gets a +2 bonus on Subterfuge when she needs to blend in.
Friends (Minor): Freckles always knows someone who can help, but she isn't necessarily on good terms with them.
Photographic Memory: Freckles never forgets a detail.
Resourceful Pockets: Freckles tends to carry whatever she needs with her, which is impressive given her small stature!
Screamer! Freckles is a screamer, but this is usually part of her act, playing the role of frightened child to attract aid and cover her escape.
Selfish: Freckles always puts her well-being first.
Sense of Direction: Freckles knows the streets of London like the spikes on her head.

TECH LEVEL: 4 STORY POINTS: 2

Freckles usually pretends to be a homeless child, although on occasion she acts as an adult of short stature instead. She typically plays the latter when she believes that Strax is around, as Freckles is a bit sweet on him, although Strax is unsurprisingly oblivious to her attention. Freckles continues to practice her criminal trade in London. She is an accomplished beggar, burglar and con artist. Given that she has few needs, Freckles generally limits herself to petty crimes, which makes it easier for the Paternoster Gang to overlook her misdemeanours in return for her help in other cases.

Freckles has an unparalleled knowledge of London's streets as well as its seamy underbelly. Freckles doesn't mind sharing information so long as the Paternoster Gang are discreet and pay for their services with a gift. She usually uses gifts to cement her relations with others, anything from an order of fish and chips from a particular shop to a coat, cut and material from a clothier on New Oxford Street. Of course, if Freckles has gotten herself into trouble, then the 'gift' may simply be helping her to get out of it!

DAME REGINA SMYTHE

The unassuming landlady of the enigmatic Diogenes Club, Dame Regina Smythe is one of the most powerful people in Great Britain. She is extremely well connected and highly placed within the government – it is said that Regina even has the Queen's ear – although she holds herself out only as an ageing, doddering dilettante who is more concerned with the condition of the club and the comfort of its members.

Her matronly manner is very soothing and she uses it to uncover secrets, broker deals and convey information. However, 'Regina Smythe' may not even be her real name and no one is quite certain how she was knighted. What is certain is that Regina has a great knowledge of the Doctor, although whether she knows him personally is a matter of debate, and she did surprise Madame Vastra once by telling her that she knew that she was a Silurian. The Diogenes Club is as mysterious as its owner – there are rumours that the interior can change, with rooms seeming to appear, disappear or change sizes at her whim.

Regina is a valuable resource to the Paternoster Gang. She represents the British Government on sensitive matters and an invitation to the Diogenes Club usually means that Her Majesty needs something dealt with discreetly. Her knowledge of history is vast (and she often speaks of historical events as if she's been there) and her library is voluminous; she can retrieve any book or periodical that a Diogenes member or Paternoster requests. Meeting with Regina is often a sure-fire way of attracting the Torchwood Institute's attention, however, so Paternosters tend to seek the Earl of Shaftfield's aid instead if they can help it.

REGINA SMYTHE

AWARENESS	3	PRESENCE	6
COORDINATION	2	RESOLVE	5
INGENUITY	5	STRENGTH	1

SKILLS

Convince 4, Knowledge 5, Medicine 3, Science 3, Subterfuge 5, Technology 4, Transport 2.

TRAITS

Brave: Regina gets a +2 bonus on Resolve rolls when she needs to show courage.
Empathic: Regina has an excellent feel for people. She gets a +2 bonus when trying to read others.
Friends (Major): Regina has powerful friends amongst the Diogenes membership as well as within the British government.
Indomitable: She gets a +4 to rolls to resist hypnosis, mind control or possession.

TECH LEVEL: 4 STORY POINTS: 2

WHO IS THE DAME?

With Dame Regina's quirks and historical knowledge, as well as the Diogenes Club's seemingly TARDIS-like traits, it's fair to ask whether the Dame is actually a Time Lord. While we've presented Regina's statistics as though she is human, you might decide otherwise. Regina could be a Time Lord who's been transformed via a Chameleon Arch, or she might be another time traveller, such as a 51st century Time Agent or a former (or future) companion of the Doctor. Whatever you decide, Regina is genuinely interested in helping Great Britain, or at least preserving history, and her arms' length approach to the Torchwood Institute makes her a powerful ally. It's not a bad tack to simply keep the players guessing, dropping hints about Regina but never telling her full story – they may surprise you by coming up with their own theory of Regina that you can steal!

FRANKLIN TUTTLE

Franklin was never meant to amount to anything, at least to hear him tell his story. The son of working class parents, Franklin was expected to join his parents toiling in a factory. He quickly grew envious of those who had more and became a prime candidate for recruitment by various social reform movements, including anarchism and communism. Franklin had a keen mind and became adept at bomb-building.

FRANKLIN TUTTLE

AWARENESS	2	PRESENCE	4
COORDINATION	3	RESOLVE	3
INGENUITY	3	STRENGTH	4

SKILLS

Athletics 3, Convince 2, Craft 5 (Demolitions 7), Fighting 4, Knowledge 2, Marksman 3, Subterfuge 3, Survival 2.

TRAITS

Brave: Franklin gets a +2 bonus to any Resolve roll when he needs to show courage.
Distinctive: Franklin takes a -2 penalty to rolls to blend in. Others have a +2 bonus to remember or recognise him.
Friends (Minor): Franklin has many friends and contacts on the street, especially those connected to anarchist and communist movements.
Impaired Senses: Blind in one eye and deaf in one ear.
Special – Demolitions Expert: Franklin is considered to be both a Boffin and Technically Adept when dealing with demolitions and explosive devices generally. He can build bombs and gets +2 bonus when doing so.
Tough: Franklin is made of tough stuff. Reduce total damage by 2.
Unattractive: Franklin's patchy appearance imposes a -2 penalty to any rolls that involve his looks. It also provides a +2 to intimidate rolls thanks to the imposing frame that goes with it.

TECH LEVEL: 4 STORY POINTS: 2

Franklin was naïve in that he thought his bombs would only be used to scare people, not to actually kill anyone. When one of his anarchist allies used one of his bombs to try to assassinate the Queen at the opera, Franklin changed sides and worked with Madame Vastra to foil the plot. Unfortunately, he was caught in his own explosion while ushering people out of the building and would have died had Strax not been there to save him. At Vastra's recommendation, the Queen pardoned him for his part in the plot.

Two years later, Franklin is an 'antiquities dealer,' which is primarily a fencing operation. As per his agreement with Vastra, Franklin continues working with his social reformist allies so long as he stops short of violent action and reports any groups that wish to do harm. Vastra has also found Franklin's talent at demolition to be useful on occasion. She actually encourages him to continue with his reformist efforts, so long as they are peaceful.

Naturally tall and big-boned, Franklin cuts an imposing figure. He bears many scars from the bomb explosion, giving his skin a patchwork appearance in many places as well as the sobriquet 'Frankenstein.' Franklin is blind in his left eye and deaf in what is left of his left ear. His hair only grows in patches on the left side of his head, so Franklin rarely takes off his bowler, even indoors.

THE PRIME MINISTER

With the exception of the Queen, one of the highest-ranking targets for anarchists, foreign agents and alien threats is the Prime Minister of Parliament. In keeping with the fluid nature of the Paternoster campaign and to avoid getting too mired in actual history, we've invented an entirely new Prime Minister who serves during a gap somewhere between the three Prime Ministers who actually held the office in the 1890s. By using a fictional Prime Minister, the Gamemaster can easily up the stakes by putting him in mortal danger without worrying about disrupting the timeline or making the players feel that his timely rescue is a fait accompli.

Nathan Fairfield, 8th Earl of Redbury, is the former Leader of the House of Lords and an imperialist. He rejects the notion of home rule in Ireland and Wales and advocates a stronger British military presence throughout the world. He is also a strong proponent of Britain maintaining 'splendid isolation' with other European powers, maintaining good relations with all of them but not allowing itself to get entangled in specific alliances with any of them. He is, however, concerned with Germany and Russia's growing power and influence.

Personally, Lord Redbury is a cheerful man who enjoys a good party. He is respectful to everyone he meets and treats even the briefest of acquaintances as if they were good friends, usually calling them by their first names (if socially appropriate). The one area where Lord Redbury is much more reserved is the notion of legacy. While young for a Prime Minister, Lord Redbury is fast approaching middle age and is still unmarried; he seems rather uninterested in finding a wife and having children. Fortunately for the Prime Minister, much of the blame seems to rest on the shoulders of his Principal Private Secretary, Sir Douglas Fairfax, who sets aside little time in the Prime Minister's taxing schedule for possible courtships.

NATHAN FAIRFIELD, 8TH EARL OF REDBURY

AWARENESS	3	PRESENCE	5
COORDINATION	3	RESOLVE	5
INGENUITY	3	STRENGTH	2

SKILLS
Convince 3 (Leadership 5), Fighting 2, Knowledge 3, Marksman 3, Subterfuge 2.

TRAITS
Charming: Lord Redbury is very personable and gets a +2 bonus on attempts to charm others.
Eccentric: Lord Redbury's mannerisms sometimes leads to occasional awkwardness in social situations.
Friends (Major): Lord Redbury has many friends within the government and the Peerage.
Noble: Lord Redbury is an earl and gets a +2 bonus on rolls with anyone with a lesser title or commoner.
Obligation (Major): Lord Redbury leads the government.
Voice of Authority: Lord Redbury gets a +2 bonus to Presence + Convince rolls.

TECH LEVEL: 4 STORY POINTS: 2

THE PRINCIPAL PRIVATE SECRETARY

Sir Douglas Fairfax is oft considered the Prime Minister's right hand; the less charitable call the secretary his gatekeeper. The baronet is a handsome man with a full head of red hair and whiskers, but is also well-known for his mood swings. This is attributed to his 'Scottish temper' even though Sir Douglas actually hails from York and has a slight Yorkshire accent. He is fiercely loyal to the Prime Minister and aggressively protects his reputation; anyone who wishes to gain an audience with the Prime Minister must first convince Sir Douglas to arrange it. Given that Lord Redbury remains unmarried there is no one closer to him than Sir Douglas and there is a joke circulating amongst the Peers that any woman who marries the Prime Minister must marry Sir Douglas as well.

The close bond between Sir Douglas and Lord Redbury is intended to be used as a gateway to the Prime Minister, both for the Paternoster Gang and their enemies. Should the Paternosters cultivate a relationship with Sir Douglas then they will gain a powerful ally within Her Majesty's Government; they offend him at their peril.

Conversely, Sir Douglas is a tempting target for enemies. He could be forcefully recruited as one of Napoleon's Chessmen (see pg. 64), he could be replaced by a Zygon or he could be tricked into granting access to the Prime Minister for some nefarious purpose. A villain could use Sir Douglas' position to operate a shadowy conspiracy right under the Prime Minister's nose!

SIR DOUGLAS FAIRFAX

AWARENESS	4	PRESENCE	3
COORDINATION	3	RESOLVE	3
INGENUITY	3	STRENGTH	3

SKILLS
Convince 3 (Bluff and Talk down 5), Fighting 2, Knowledge 3, Marksman 2, Subterfuge 3.

TRAITS
Attractive: Sir Douglas is very handsome; he gets +2 on social rolls involving his good looks.
Brave: Sir Douglas gets a +2 bonus to any Resolve roll when he needs to show courage.
Friends (Major): Sir Douglas has many friends within the government and the gentry.
Noble: As a member of the gentry, Sir Douglas gets a +2 on social rolls against commoners.
Obligation (Major): Sir Douglas is always 'on call' for the Prime Minister.
Resourceful Pockets: Sir Douglas anticipates the Prime Minister's needs and always seems to have whatever is called for on hand. Sir Douglas may roll two dice and get a 'double' (or spend a Story Point) to find something he needs.

TECH LEVEL: 4 STORY POINTS: 2

ROGUES' GALLERY

The Doctor once said that you can judge a man by the quality of his enemies. If so, then the Paternoster Gang is colourful indeed! Here is a sampling of the various villains, rogues and ne'er-do-wells that are likely to run afoul of the Paternoster Gang at some point in the near future.

In addition to providing a cast of colourful adversaries for the characters in your own game to encounter, these rogues also illustrate examples of how to use individual aliens outside of the typical 'invading army' mode. In many ways these rogues are the mirror opposites of Paternosters; individual aliens who blend into Victorian society in order to manipulate it rather than protect it. And remember, once the Paternoster Gang has dealt with a particular alien rogue there is always another waiting to fill the vacuum left behind!

As with the Irregulars, each rogue is given a standard number of Story Points based on their presumed importance in a given adventure. Minor rogues or henchmen have 3 Story Points, major rogues or lieutenants have 6 Story Points, while special rogues or 'bosses' have 9 Story Points. Feel free to adjust these totals if you intend a given rogue is going to play a larger or smaller role in a particular adventure.

THE ARTFUL DODGER

When Charles Dickens wrote about Fagin and his child criminals in Oliver Twist, his writings weren't entirely fictional. The true 'Artful Dodger' is a mysterious man with boundless youthful energy who takes care of London's forgotten children and teaches them how to survive, albeit by stealing from others. Over the last couple of decades, he has established a few 'ragged schools' (charities that provide free education for poor children) that are secretly funded by the illicit activities of its pupils.

The Artful Dodger used to go by the name of Sam Swift the Quick, an English highwayman from the 17th century. Sam was almost killed by Me when she used an amulet to open a portal to another part of the galaxy where an invading army was waiting. Realising that she had been duped by her supposed ally Leandro, Me gave Sam her second immortality chip, closing the portal. He was saved, but it was unknown whether the chip granted him immortality or simply restored the rest of his natural life.

In truth, it was neither. Two centuries on Sam Swift still ages, but at a snail's pace. Every few years he finds a new grey hair and Me, on the rare occasions their paths cross, notices that he's getting older. It will likely be another few centuries before he's appreciably aged. Unlike Me, the Artful Dodger doesn't heal quickly and he fears that if he were killed then his death would be permanent. As a result, Sam is very careful in his actions and, in dangerous situations, prefers to send others in his stead.

While still a criminal rogue, the Artful Dodger truly cares about the well-being of his 'raggedy children.' He instructs them in the criminal arts but discourages them from violent crimes – they are limited to burglary, pick-pocketing and confidence schemes.

Because of this his children are rarely punished too onerously if caught; often a little palm-greasing is all it takes to spring them from the cells. The Artful Dodger steals primarily to support his schools and to live comfortably. Me is content to let him be so long as he doesn't draw too much attention to them both.

SAM SWIFT

AWARENESS	4	PRESENCE	4
COORDINATION	4	RESOLVE	5
INGENUITY	5	STRENGTH	3

SKILLS

Athletics 3, Convince 5, Craft 2, Fighting 3, Knowledge 3 (London 5), Marksman 5, Medicine 2, Subterfuge 5, Survival 5, Transport 2.

TRAITS

Attractive: The Artful Dodger is a handsome rogue and gets a +2 bonus to any rolls that involve his looks.
Brave: He gets a +2 bonus to any Resolve roll when he needs to show courage.
Charming: The Artful Dodger gets a +2 bonus to attempts to use charm.
Face in the Crowd: He gets a +2 to any Subterfuge Skill roll to sneak about.
Forgetful (Minor): There's only so much room in his head for memories, so the Artful Dodger takes a -2 penalty to any Ingenuity + Resolve roll to remember something vital.
Lucky: The Artful Dodger may re-roll any 'double 1s'
Run for your Life! +1 bonus to his Speed when the Artful Dodger is escaping pursuit.
Selfish: While somewhat altruistic towards his pupils, the Artful Dodger still puts himself first in any dangerous situation, rationalising to himself that he can make everything better later.
Time Traveller: While technically he's taken the long way round, the Artful Dodger is familiar with Tech Level 3 and 4.
Unadventurous: Because of what the Artful Dodger sees as his 'fragility,' he prefers to remain in the shadows and let his pupils carry out his schemes.
Voice of Authority: The Artful Dodger gets a +2 bonus to Presence + Convince rolls.

TECH LEVEL: 4 **STORY POINTS:** 9

MISS ANNIE

Ann Benson, who is known as 'Miss Annie' amongst the Raggedy Children, was originally a raggedy girl herself and her relationship with the children and the Artful Dodger has evolved over the years as she became a raggedy leader, den mother and schoolteacher as she grew older. Her fondness for the Artful Dodger has also grown from daughter-like loyalty to something more, although the Artful Dodger pretends not to notice her attentions. In truth, the Artful Dodger fears letting anyone get close due to his seeming immortality, but he has not shared that concern with Miss Annie. For now, she remains his chief lieutenant, although anyone noticing the torch she carries could use it to turn her against him.

MISS ANNIE

AWARENESS	3	PRESENCE	4
COORDINATION	3	RESOLVE	3
INGENUITY	3	STRENGTH	2

SKILLS

Athletics 2, Convince 3, Fighting 2, Knowledge 3, Marksman 1, Medicine 1, Subterfuge 3, Survival 2.

TRAITS

Attractive: Miss Annie gets a +2 bonus to any rolls that involve her looks.
Charming: A +2 bonus to her attempts to use charm.
Code of Conduct: The Artful Dodger has taught her to refrain from violent actions.
Empathic: Miss Annie gets a +2 bonus on rolls to 'read' another person.
Sense of Direction: A +2 bonus to any navigation roll
Voice of Authority: Miss Annie gets a +2 bonus to Presence and Convince rolls.

TECH LEVEL: 4 **STORY POINTS:** 6

RAGGEDY CHILDREN

AWARENESS	4	PRESENCE	2
COORDINATION	3	RESOLVE	3
INGENUITY	2	STRENGTH	1

SKILLS

Athletics 2, Convince 2, Fighting 1, Subterfuge 3, Survival 2.

TRAITS

Code of Conduct: A raggedy child finds it hard to do bad.
Empathic: A raggedy child gets a +2 bonus on rolls to 'read' another person.
Face in the Crowd: +2 to any Subterfuge Skill roll to sneak about.
Run for your Life: A raggedy child gets a +1 bonus to your Speed when escaping pursuit.
Screamer: Spend a Story Point to stun anything or anyone else in the room for one action.
Sense of Direction: A raggedy child gets a +2 bonus to any navigation roll.

TECH LEVEL: 4 STORY POINTS: 3

LEPER HALL

Leper Hall is a large building in the vicinity of Covent Garden, a neighbourhood dominated by brothels, coffee houses, markets, taverns and theatres. While it dominates an entire street front, there are few who do more than rush past it on their way to more pleasurable experiences. Leper Hall has a reputation of admitting diseased patients who are never seen again and some wrongly believe that simply standing near the building risks exposure to leprosy and other diseases. No, Leper Hall is quite left alone by Londoners and its immortal owner likes it that way.

Leper Hall was founded by Me, under the alias of 'Alice Shield,' as a sanctuary for aliens stranded on Earth. She had owned the estate for quite some time, using it as a base of operations, but felt a change was in order after Covent Garden became a red light district. Her friendship with Lewis Carroll (see pg. 13) provided her with a name based on both word play and double entendre – 'Leper Hall' is a corruption of 'Lepus Hole' or 'Rabbit Hole,' implying that Leper Hall isn't all that it seems (Me is coy if asked whether she influenced *Alice's Adventures in Wonderland* or if it was the other way around). The name also misidentifies the sanctuary as a leper hospital, keeping people from prying too much into its comings and goings.

While actually the owner of the estate, Me poses as its head nurse, preferring that most visitors perceive the steward Hester Biggs as the true authority. The hall is actually quite expansive: it's a four-storey building surrounding a beautifully landscaped courtyard, and there is even an indoor swimming pool. Several rooms are converted to accommodate the specific needs of aliens that aren't comfortable in human environments. When not in their quarters, all aliens are expected to wear their holographic emitters to appear human.

Me strictly maintains Leper Hall's secrecy. She identifies aliens on her own (or with help from others in the know, such as Madame Vastra or Sam Swift) and offers them a chance to live the rest of their lives free from worry in return for following the strict rules of Leper Hall. Those that accept the offer fall under Hester Bigg's jurisdiction; those that don't are never told specifics about Leper Hall. Only in rare instances has Me taken hostile action when someone threatens to expose the sanctuary.

Me, and by extension Leper Hall, hinders the Paternoster Gang as often as she helps them. Should Me snatch an alien in the midst of an investigation the alien will gain the equivalent of diplomatic immunity and Me will need to be convinced that giving the Paternosters access would do more good than harm. Hester Biggs has a tendency to hunt down and terminate rule breakers regardless of whether the Paternoster Gang have had a chance to question them or not.

'ALICE SHIELD'

Alice Shield is an immortal, having lived for a thousand years. She began life as Ashildr, a Norse girl whose village was attacked by the alien warriors known as the Mire. The Doctor and Clara arrived and set things right, but Ashildr was killed in the process . The Doctor saved her life by using a Mire medical chip to resuscitate her, but the chip also made her effectively immortal. She would never grow old.

Unfortunately, Ashildr's immortality did not give her an immortal-sized brain to go with it and she found herself continually forgetting things no longer relevant to her and had reinvented herself so many times that she forgot her original name, referring to herself simply as "Me". While she began keeping a library of journals to remind her of her experiences, she became emotionally detached. She gave up on love and family after watching too many lovers age and die and losing her own children to a plague. Me turned to criminal activity to ease her boredom and, in the 17th century, almost sparked an alien invasion when an alien convinced her that he could take her to the stars if she helped him open a portal. This event shocked her into realising that she still cared about life.

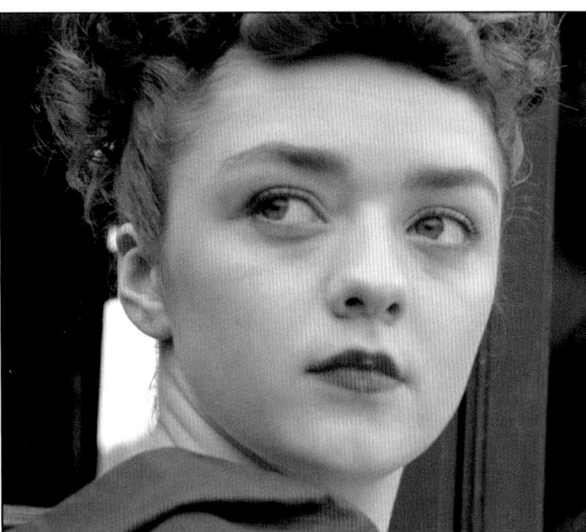

Me was given a second medical chip by the Doctor when she was first revived. He'd expected her to use it on someone she loved so that she might have an immortal companion, but she never found anyone worth committing to (or that she hadn't already grown bored with). She ended up using the chip to save highwayman Sam Swift, who she'd mortally wounded to open the alien portal. When the Doctor refused to take Me with her to travel time and space, Me pledged instead to protect the world from the consequences of the Doctor's meddling.

Me's vow has resulted in her collecting aliens, most of whom were left abandoned on Earth after the Doctor thwarted their plans. Currently she is housing them in her London estate, Leper Hall, where she masquerades as Alice Shield, a head nurse. She has also adapted her former criminal disguise as the Knightmare, travelling through the city at night in a carriage wearing a cloak, hat and mask. It is in this guise, usually with Hester and Korval in tow, that she interviews prospective tenants for Leper Hall.

Whilst she would never admit it, Me is terrified of Napoleon. She isn't quite sure what he is, but she knows he is alien and that if she draws too much attention to Leper Hall he might kill everyone. She is careful to tread carefully around Napoleon's schemes and pulls back whenever she feels his tendrils.

ME

AWARENESS	3	PRESENCE	5
COORDINATION	4	RESOLVE	4
INGENUITY	5	STRENGTH	3

SKILLS
Athletics 3, Convince 4, Fighting 3, Knowledge 5, Marksman 3, Subterfuge 4, Survival 4, Technology 2, Transport 3.

TRAITS
Alien: The use of a Mire chip effectively makes Me an alien hybrid.
Arrogant: Me believes herself to be above others, gaining +2 to resist fear but suffering -1 in social situations with her perceived inferiors.
Dark Secret: Both Me's immortal nature and Leper Hall's existence could make life problematic for her if discovered.
Face in the Crowd: Me's young, innocent appearance makes her easy to overlook.
Fast Healing (Major)
Forgetful (Minor): Occasionally, Me deletes something from her brain that would have been helpful. She takes a -2 penalty to any Ingenuity + Resolve roll to remember something vital.
Immortal: Me cannot die. Even if killed, her Mire chip repairs her.
Obligation (Minor): Me sees herself as the caretaker to the aliens of Leper Hall.
Outsider: Me's nature makes it difficult for her to form friendships and she suffers a -2 penalty to her rolls when trying to develop them.
Run for your Life! Me is used to running away from situations and has become quite adept at it.
Selfish: Me's aloof nature and immortal perspective often make her seem selfish.
Time Traveller: Me is taking the slow approach to time travel, but is (so far) familiar with Tech Levels 2 to 4.
Unadventurous: Me is bored with life and travel. It's difficult for her to get excited about seeing something new on this world.

TECH LEVEL: 4 STORY POINTS: 9

HESTER BIGGS

Hester Biggs, the steward of Leper Hall, is remarkable for two reasons. The first, of course, is that she is a steward in spite of being a woman. The second, and even more remarkable fact, is that she is an alien. In fact, Hester Biggs is a Judoon, and in addition to being the steward of Leper Hall she is also its primary law enforcement official.

Hester originally came to the solar system on assignment to stop an 'illegal' salvage mission to Mars. When her quarry panicked, the criminal accidentally activated an Ice Warrior defence system that disabled Hester's vessel and sent it plunging towards Earth. Hester and two of her team survived.

Me offered Hester and her remaining crew sanctuary in Leper Hall while they await a rescue expedition. Hester became the steward, or chief security officer, while her two subordinates pose as orderlies.

Unlike the other residents of Leper Hall, Hester and her crew's contract is at-will for both parties; Hester and her crew can leave at any time. As it turns out, Hester rather enjoys her role and has rescinded her request for a rescue, preferring to remain on Earth. She has yet to mention this to her crew and it's possible that either of them may mutiny, especially if someone else can offer them passage home.

HESTER BIGGS

AWARENESS	3	PRESENCE	4
COORDINATION	2	RESOLVE	5
INGENUITY	3	STRENGTH	8

SKILLS
Athletics 1, Convince 3, Fighting 3, Knowledge 3 (Law 5), Marksman 3, Subterfuge 2, Survival 2, Technology 2, Transport 3.

TRAITS
Alien
Alien Appearance (Major)
Armour (Minor): Hester usually wears her Judoon armour, which enables her to reduce injury by 5 levels.
By the Book: Hester follows Me's orders to the letter. She terminates any alien who fails to follow the Cheshire rules.
Code of Conduct: Uphold the law.
Fear Factor (2): In her natural form, Hester is very intimidating and gets a +4 to rolls when actively trying to intimidate. When she is disguised as a human, Hester retains this bonus to those who know her true nature.
Slow (Minor): Hester is heavy and armoured; her Speed is only 1. Her holographic emitter takes account of this by projecting a slight limp.
Special – Lung Capacity: Hester has a large lung capacity, allowing her to survive without air, or within a poisonous environment, for far longer than a human. She does not need to make any rolls to survive without air unless in incredibly prolonged circumstances.
Time Traveller (Minor): Tech Level 4.
Voice of Authority: Hester's commanding voice and her nature as a Judoon grants her a +2 to Presence + Convince rolls.

EQUIPMENT
Blaster (4/L/L)
Holographic Emitter (Minor Gadget): In sharp contrast to her true appearance, Hester appears to be a sweet, fragile human approaching middle age. Occasionally the guise falls for a half-second, revealing her true nature, but this tends to happen only in stressful situations where the gadget has trouble compensating for jerky movements. See pg. 60.
Translator/Scanner (Major Gadget): Translate (any language), Scan (Medical)

TECH LEVEL: 6 STORY POINTS: 6

KORVAL

One of Me's most trusted underlings is Korval, a Graske who was infiltrating Earth in preparation for an alien invasion when he was stopped by the Doctor. Understanding that Korval was simply a pawn, albeit a somewhat willing one, the Doctor took pity on him, limiting Korval's ability to teleport and shift dimensions.

With a mind conditioned for loyalty, Korval was an easy recruit for Me. He serves her without question, using his skills as a messenger, scout, spy, or a 'fetcher' as needed. In the latter case he stuns or immobilises a potential alien recruit long enough for Me to interview them. Korval typically appears as a street beggar, but he assumes other forms as needed.

KORVAL

AWARENESS	4	PRESENCE	3
COORDINATION	3	RESOLVE	2
INGENUITY	4	STRENGTH	2

SKILLS
Athletics 2, Convince 2, Fighting 3, Knowledge 3, Marksman 3, Subterfuge 5, Survival 1, Technology 2, Transport 2.

TRAITS
Alien
Alien Appearance
Enslaved: While Me doesn't treat Korval any differently to the other members of Leper Hall, Korval has a submissive personality and considers her words sacrosanct.
Face in the Crowd: In his human guise, Korval is adept at making himself blend in. He gets a +2 to Subterfuge rolls.
Shapeshift (Minor): Korval can assume any form he chooses. He uses this trait instead of a holographic emitter.
Time Traveller (Minor): Tech Level 4.

EQUIPMENT
Dimension Gun: Korval's gun is not as powerful as a typical Graske weapon, but it still has the following settings:

- Stun a target
- Freeze a target in time (temporarily) lasting 60 (30/60/90) seconds

TECH LEVEL: 6 STORY POINTS: 3

NEW GADGET – HOLOGRAPHIC EMITTER (MAJOR GADGET)

Based on various alien technologies that Me has managed to salvage, the holographic emitter enables the wearer to appear human. It also enables the wearer to speak and understand English. Unfortunately, the holographic emitter works best when the subject is calm or in normal situations. If the subject is excited or surprised then the holographic emitter may momentarily glitch while compensating, exposing the subject's true nature. Anyone looking at the subject when this happens notices the change if they succeed at a Ingenuity + Presence roll (Difficulty 6; the difficulty may be raised the further away the observer is).

Traits: Innocuous, Shapeshift (Minor Good), Transmit (Language), Special – Glitch (Minor Bad)
Story Points: 2

THE NAPOLEON OF CRIME

Napoleon is a shadowy individual who has his tendrils in every criminal element in London and throughout the British Empire. He prefers to operate in the shadows and no one, including his perennial nemesis Madame Vastra, knows who he is. The answer is as chilling as it is enigmatic: the Napoleon of Crime is a Dalek.

Napoleon has been stranded in London for almost three decades thanks to a local time cabinet built by Professors Maxtible and Waterfield in 1867. The combination of reflective mirrors and nearby Dalek Time Corridor technology inadvertently created a temporal window into the Last Great Time War and Napoleon was caught in the resulting time bubble. When Waterfield's house exploded, the mirrors shattered and Napoleon was freed into the confusion that was Victorian England.

Fortunately for him, Napoleon was a master strategist; indeed, his role during the Time War was assessing threats and minimising losses. Thus, rather than announce his presence to the world he quickly retreated into the shadows where he could more accurately analyse his situation and figure out how to get back to the war; he is unaware of the time lock put in place by the Doctor. Napoleon used the construction of the London Underground

NAPOLEON

AWARENESS	4	PRESENCE	6
COORDINATION	2	RESOLVE	5
INGENUITY	6	STRENGTH	7*

SKILLS
Convince 5, Fighting 4, Knowledge 5, Marksman 3, Medicine 3, Science 8, Subterfuge 4, Survival 4, Technology 8.

TRAITS
Armour (Major): The Dalekanium casing reduces damage by 10. This does reduce Napoleon's Coordination to 2 (already included in his Attributes).
Boffin (Major): Napoleon can create Gadgets.
Cyborg
Dark Secret (Major): Napoleon takes great pains to conceal his true nature. Should Madame Vastra or the Torchwood Institute learn this they would most certainly triple their efforts to capture or destroy him.
Environmental (Major): Napoleon can survive in the vacuum of space, underwater or other hostile environments.
Fear Factor (4): No one who has faced Napoleon can consider him anything less than terrifying. He gets a +8 to rolls when actively scaring someone.
Flight (Major): Napoleon can fly. When hovering his Speed is effectively 1, when in open skies or space he has a Speed of 6.
Forcefield (Major): Bullets appear to stop in the air before Napoleon, appearing to dissolve on contact with his powerful forcefield. Damage is reduced by two levels (from Disastrous to Failure, from Bad to Success, and so on).
Indomitable (Major): Napoleon gets a +4 bonus to any rolls to resist psychic control.
Natural Weapon – Exterminator: The Dalek weapon usually kills with a single shot (4/L/L).
Networked: Napoleon is networked to Mister Steele and the Chessmen.
Scan: While scarce in Victorian London, Napoleon can interface with computers. He can also interface with living beings to learn new information; while not necessarily lethal, Napoleon usually kills his victim after such extractions to prevent reprisals (4/L/L).
Special – Self Destruct: While loathe to do so, Napoleon retains the capacity to self-destruct, causing (3/6/9) levels of damage to those within 10m of the explosion.
Technically Adept: Napoleon is brilliant at using and adapting technology.
Time Traveller (Minor): Napoleon is familiar with Tech Level 4.
Voice of Authority: Napoleon's grating voice makes him particularly effective when barking orders to those not used to hearing 'machines.' He gets a +2 bonus to Presence and Convince rolls when issuing orders.
Wanted (Minor): Napoleon has a criminal reputation. Given that he is well-protected and the police are usually focused on those on the outer edge of Napoleon's empire, this is only a Minor Bad trait.

*Napoleon has different attributes when removed from his Dalekanium casing. Movement outside of the armour is incredibly limited (Speed 1) and he will not survive very long. If the mutant is exposed at any time, damage inflicted to Napoleon may bypass the armour.

AWARENESS	3	PRESENCE	4
COORDINATION	3	RESOLVE	4
INGENUITY	6	STRENGTH	5

SKILLS: As above.

TRAITS: **Boffin (Major), Climbing (Minor), Dark Secret (Major), Fear Factor (4), Immunity (Radiation), Indomitable (Major), Natural Weapons (Minor) – Tentacles (2/5/7), Technically Adept, Alien Appearance (Major), Slow (Minor), Voice of Authority (Minor), Wanted (Minor).**

TECH LEVEL: 9 STORY POINTS: 12

to create a secret base from where he could watch from the shadows and recruit aid. He discovered the remnants of Cyber-technology that the government kept in local warehouses in the wake of an earlier Cyber-invasion. Napoleon arranged for some of it to be stolen so that he could repurpose it.

As the years marched on Napoleon grew more cunning, aided by his ability to absorb knowledge from captured criminals, whose minds he's 'processed' in order to learn new criminal methods. Napoleon's ultimate goal is to re-join his brethren in the Time War and towards that end he is trying to build his own Time Corridor. To do that he needs to ensure that certain technologies are developed so that he can acquire the necessary components. Napoleon understands that this is a long game but he has time to wait. He has built a criminal empire to aid him in his endeavours and most of his underlings do not realise who they are really working for, especially since Napoleon tends to operate through his lieutenant, Mister Steele.

Other than his desire to return to war, there are two things that shape Napoleon's actions. The first is his knowledge of future history; Napoleon knows that the Daleks conquer Earth in another two centuries and disrupting the timeline might give the Time Lords an advantage (the fact that the invasion failed is of little consequence – it plays a role in Dalek history and Napoleon is cautious not to create temporal ripples).

The second thing is that – in spite of his nature – Napoleon actually enjoys being a criminal mastermind. He is still the consummate strategist and having a nemesis to challenge him invigorates him. He sees Madame Vastra as a worthy opponent and has recently styled himself as "the Napoleon of Crime" as the counterpoint to Vastra's "consulting detective". Interestingly, Strax has remarked on more than one occasion that the enigmatic Napoleon sometimes unnecessarily puts his own plans in jeopardy. There is some truth to this; Napoleon enjoys the game so much that there's a part of him that would rather remain in Victorian London rather than return to the Time War. If she ever discovered the truth Vastra might even find that endearing if it weren't for the fact that, when all is said and done, Napoleon is still a Dalek.

MISTER STEELE

Mister Steele is a man re-invented in more ways than one. None of his associates know his true background and Mister Steele never refers to his life before becoming Napoleon's right-hand man. The only clues are contradictory: Mister Steele speaks with a cockney accent unless angered, in which case he curses in French. He bears many scars; some of these are due to the upgrades he's received but most are older, suggesting a violent past. His previously broken nose and knowledge of fisticuffs have led some to conclude that Mister Steele was once a bare-knuckle boxer.

MISTER STEELE

AWARENESS	3	PRESENCE	5
COORDINATION	4	RESOLVE	4
INGENUITY	2	STRENGTH	7

SKILLS
Athletics 4, Convince 3, Fighting 4, Marksman 3, Subterfuge 4, Survival 3.

TRAITS
Armour (Minor Trait): The plate grafts beneath Mister Steele's skin reduce any damage he takes by 5.
Arrogance: Mister Steele's own sense of worth and his upgrades make him feel superior to everyone around him (and this is only getting worse as the Cyber-programming asserts control). He gains a +2 to resist fear and feelings of hopelessness, but suffers -1 to social interactions with those he considers inferior.
Cyborg
Dark Secret: Mister Steele's Cyber-programming is in the early stages of asserting control. Should Napoleon discover this he will quickly exterminate Mister Steele.
Distinctive: Mister Steele is a hulking brute who stands out in a crowd.
Eccentric: In spite of being a criminal thug, Mister Steele has refined tastes.
Natural Weapon – Electric Grip: Mister Steele can generate an electric pulse from his hand, increasing his damage in close combat to (4/9/13).
Networked: Mister Steele is wirelessly networked to Napoleon and the Chessmen.
Obligation (Major): Mister Steele feels intense loyalty to Napoleon.
Quick Reflexes (Minor): Mister Steele usually acts first in a round.
Tough (Minor): Mister Steele's own physical toughness reduces any damage he takes by 2, in addition to his armour.

TECH LEVEL: 4 **STORY POINTS:** 6

In any event, the physically imposing Mister Steele has become an unwavering lieutenant to Napoleon and is responsible for carrying out and overseeing Napoleon's grander plans. At times Mister Steele even takes the blame for revealed crimes in order to protect his master. He's worked this scheme so well that many, including some within the organisation, believe that Mister Steele is the Napoleon of Crime who simply maintains the fiction of an even higher master. Of course, Napoleon is real and is responsible for Mister Steele's current form. The Dalek took a broken man and repaired him with scavenged Cyber-technology in return for his unquestioning service. Mister Steele doesn't understand exactly what he is but he enjoys the power the technology grants him. He feels freer to indulge in expensive passions such as eating at fine establishments or going to the opera, even though he tends to stick out like a sore thumb.

While Mister Steele seems the consummate lieutenant, there is one dangerous aspect to him – his Cyber-programming. Unbeknownst to Napoleon, the Dalek wasn't able to wipe away pre-existing orders implanted within the technology by the Cyber-King. The nanotech chips containing these orders are slowly repairing themselves and rewiring Mister Steele's brain. This is causing Mister Steele to make preparations to build a new, more powerful Cyber-King, and to upgrade all of London into Cybermen right under Napoleon's nose. Thus far these preparations are in the early stages and Mister Steele is trying to fight, or at least placate, these urges. He doesn't want to betray Napoleon, but he is smart enough to know what's likely to happen if he should share this 'defect' with his master.

MISS LOVELACE

While Napoleon has no reason – yet – to suspect treachery on the part of Mister Steele, he does understand that the best way to keep him honest is to have a rival. Although, none of the Chessmen were capable of rising to the occasion, Napoleon struck upon a new opportunity when his agents found that Scotland Yard had acquired the components from several Clockwork Robots. While the Torchwood Institute commandeered the lion's share, Napoleon's agents 'acquired' an almost complete robot – Miss Lovelace.

Using scavenged technologies Napoleon was able to give Miss Lovelace an independent power source and, by extension, an independent personality. She was able to rebuild herself by lurking in the worst parts of London and stealing the fleshy 'parts' she needed, often with fatal results for the donor. As a result, Miss Lovelace is becoming more and more 'human,' although at her core she is still a Clockwork Robot.

MISS LOVELACE

AWARENESS	3	PRESENCE	4
COORDINATION	3	RESOLVE	4
INGENUITY	4	STRENGTH	5

SKILLS
Athletics 3, Convince 3, Fighting 4, Knowledge 3, Marksman 2, Medicine 4, Science 2, Subterfuge 2, Technology 5, Transport 1.

TRAITS
Boffin (Major): As with all of her kind, Miss Lovelace can create Gadgets and repair herself, freely adapting organic and inorganic matter.
Natural Weapons – Retractable Blades: Miss Lovelace is equipped with hidden tools that have been refashioned into retractable blades. She adds +2 to her Strength when determining damage. She can also run an electric current through them (an adaptation of Cyber-technology) that increases the damage by another +2 (5/7/9).
Networked (Major): Miss Lovelace has complete telepathic contact with other Clockwork Robots.
Cyborg: Miss Lovelace began life as a robot, but she's grafted on so many biological parts that it is difficult to distinguish woman from machine.
Scan (Minor)
Technically Adept (Minor): Miss Lovelace is good at fixing things, even with seemingly incompatible parts. She gets a +2 to any Technology roll to fix a broken or faulty device.
Teleport (Major): Miss Lovelace can shift to another known location with an Awareness + Resolve roll. Failure just means she doesn't move.

TECH LEVEL: 6 STORY POINTS: 6

In her short time as an independent 'robot', Miss Lovelace is trying to learn to be more human, but she doesn't quite understand emotions. While she has a pleasant enough personality – social decorum demands it – she can be cold and ruthless if she doesn't get her way.

What she wants most of all is to please Napoleon, and she never misses an opportunity to rib Mister Steele, who she sees as ham-handed and mysterious in equal measure. Napoleon enjoys the growing rivalry between them and sees it as a game; man turned machine against machine turned woman.

CHESSMEN

Napoleon considers his preparations to build a Time Corridor and his run-ins with Madame Vastra and the police to all be part of his 'great game.' This game includes committing crimes and investing in particular industrial endeavours in order to create the technology that Napoleon needs. It also creates a need for numerous pawns or, in Napoleon's parlance, Chessmen.

Chessmen are created along the same lines as Dalek Puppets, save that, like Mister Steele, they are created from a mixture of Cyber-technology, Clockwork Robot and other alien technologies that Napoleon has found along the way.

CHESSMEN

AWARENESS	3	PRESENCE	2
COORDINATION	2	RESOLVE	3
INGENUITY	2	STRENGTH	4

SKILLS
Athletics 2, Fighting 3, Marksman 3, Transport 2.

TRAITS
Cyborg
Armour (Minor): Reduce damage by 5.
Enslaved (Major): A Chessman's programming ensures that he must obey Napoleon and he suffers -2 to attempts to voice contrary opinions.
Networked: Chessmen are wirelessly networked to each other, Mister Steele and Napoleon.

TECH LEVEL: 4 STORY POINTS: 2

CYBERSHADE

Cybershades are 'upgraded' versions of animals (or, more accurately, different animals grafted together) that are given cybernetic parts. While the original Cybershades were destroyed in London in 1851, Napoleon has unlocked the secrets to their

creation and has enlisted the aid of the Borad in creating new Cybershades. While Napoleon still prefers to use his Chessmen for more delicate activities, he enjoys employing his Cybershades as shock troops.

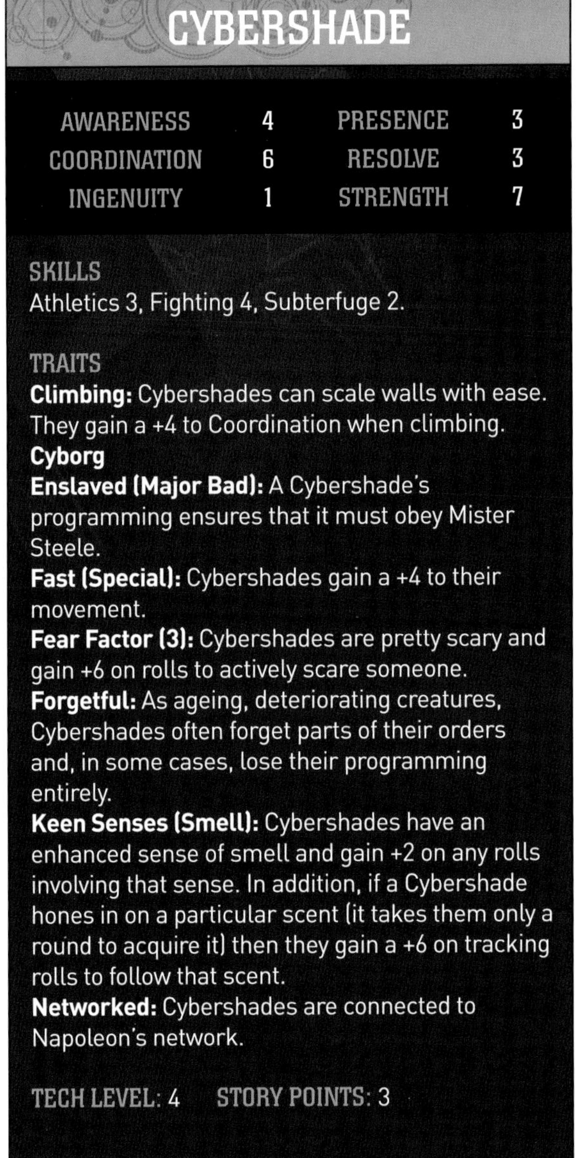

CYBERSHADE

AWARENESS	4	PRESENCE	3
COORDINATION	6	RESOLVE	3
INGENUITY	1	STRENGTH	7

SKILLS
Athletics 3, Fighting 4, Subterfuge 2.

TRAITS
Climbing: Cybershades can scale walls with ease. They gain a +4 to Coordination when climbing.
Cyborg
Enslaved (Major Bad): A Cybershade's programming ensures that it must obey Mister Steele.
Fast (Special): Cybershades gain a +4 to their movement.
Fear Factor (3): Cybershades are pretty scary and gain +6 on rolls to actively scare someone.
Forgetful: As ageing, deteriorating creatures, Cybershades often forget parts of their orders and, in some cases, lose their programming entirely.
Keen Senses (Smell): Cybershades have an enhanced sense of smell and gain +2 on any rolls involving that sense. In addition, if a Cybershade hones in on a particular scent (it takes them only a round to acquire it) then they gain a +6 on tracking rolls to follow that scent.
Networked: Cybershades are connected to Napoleon's network.

TECH LEVEL: 4 STORY POINTS: 3

THE REVENANT REVEREND

There are those who go to church out of duty, there are those who go to pray, and there are those who are looking for inspiration. Amongst the latter there are whispers that, sometimes, such inspiration comes not from the Divine, but rather a ghostly presence that haunts the cloisters and the naves, a shadowy priest that seems to belong yet no one knows him – or, at least, they don't remember him. He is the Revenant Reverend.

London is a very important, perhaps *the* most important, city in the world for the Silence, an intergalactic order founded to destroy the Doctor. Their plans included direct assassination of the Doctor as well as guiding Earth's technological advance to create the weapons they needed for that purpose. The most potent tool in the arsenal of the Silence are the Silents, genetically engineered confessional priests. Given that the Silents are able to plant hypnotic suggestions and the tendency for those who see them to forget the encounter, they make for a powerful adversary indeed – or they would be, if not for several hurdles late Victorian London presents for them.

First and foremost, London is positively brimming with aliens, many of whom know about the Silents. Unwilling to take chances, these aliens tend to shoot and kill Silents on sight rather than risk manipulation. Secondly, and for the Silents rather more troubling, is that Napoleon is a Dalek. During the Battle of Trenzalore, the Daleks developed defences against the Silents, including the ability to remember them. Both of these factors combined have wiped out most of the Silents that were operating in London.

The Revenant Reverend is an exception; he has adapted to the situation. He retreated into the churches – a comfortable position for one who was created as a priest – and has crafted vestments that act as psychic paper. Anyone viewing the Revenant Reverend believes him to be a calm, smiling priest, whom they forget is there the moment they turn away (although they remember him as belonging the moment they see him again!).

FATHER EDWARD

AWARENESS	4	PRESENCE	4
COORDINATION	2	RESOLVE	5
INGENUITY	3	STRENGTH	6

SKILLS

Athletics 1, Convince 5, Fighting 1, Knowledge 3, Marksman 3, Science 3, Subterfuge 5, Survival 2, Technology 5.

TRAITS

Alien

Alien Appearance

Fear Factor (2): A Silent is a scary and imposing sight to behold, often freezing its victims in fear. It gets a +4 bonus on rolls to actively scare its victims.

Hypnosis (Major): The Silents are able to plant hypnotic suggestions into a victim's subconscious mind when the target is looking at them, with a +3 bonus to their roll.

Natural Weapon (Major) – Electricity: A Silent is able to absorb even the smallest amount of electricity from the atmosphere, amplify it and discharging it from their hands as a devastating blast (4/L/L).

Special – Memory Proof: The Silents have a powerful ability to be instantly forgotten the moment the witness looks away. There is no resistance to this effect short of using an Eye Drive to constantly remind the viewer of their existence.

Technically Adept: While the Silents have no technological developments of their own, they are technological parasites and can steal and adapt existing technology to their own needs. They receive a +2 bonus to Technology rolls.

Time Traveller (Minor): Tech Level 4.

Tough: Shooting at a Silent will slow it down, but it may take multiple hits to actually stop it. Reduce any damage sustained by 2.

TECH LEVEL: 8 STORY POINTS: 6

This particular Silent has discovered that churches are a good place to lurk if one wants to plant suggestions in people in powerful places, free from the prying eyes of other aliens. Currently, he is using certain people as his eyes and ears to gather intelligence on the Doctor and his allies. He picks and chooses his targets carefully, as Napoleon's Chessmen are a constant threat and there are a few who aren't fooled by the 'psychic vestments.'

While the Revenant Reverend is an enemy of the Doctor and often behind plots to kill him – which includes manipulating the Paternoster Gang – he can also be an occasional ally. The Silent does not want anyone else interrupting his ultimate goals and he occasionally whispers helpful advice to those who come to his church for guidance. Of course, often the Paternoster Gang don't realise where they've gotten their sudden moment of inspiration from...

Napoleon, a student of art (theft), has dubbed the Silent 'Father Edward', having noted the similarity between the figure portrayed in Edvard Munch's *The Scream* and the actual form of Revenant Reverend. To Napoleon's delight 'Father Edward' has accepted the sobriquet, although the Silent sees it more as a taunting signature whenever he disrupts the Dalek's plans.

SCARLETT VALENTIN

Scarlett Valentin is the toast of Paris and an internationally renowned opera singer and actress. Her beauty is unparalleled in the theatre circuit and she has the voice of an angel. There isn't a court in Europe for whom she hasn't performed and she has done many tours abroad as well.

Currently, Scarlett is performing at the Savoy Theatre, playing the role of Yum-Yum in *The Mikado*. Thanks in large part to Scarlett's popularity every performance is sold out and there is a rather lucrative black market for getting tickets – Scarlett often uses this system to extract favours in return for tickets. There is an air of arrogance about Scarlett that most dismiss as the prerogative of a beautiful, successful actress, but they would be wrong. The truth is that Scarlett really does feel superior to everyone around her, as she is actually an alien who is far older than anyone she meets.

Scarlett Valentin is actually Scaroth, the last of the Jagaroth and the purported saviour of her race. Scaroth was an engineer on the last surviving Jagaroth ship and came to primordial Earth to determine its suitability as a colony world. It was not, and against Scaroth's advice the ship tried to take off with a damaged warp drive. The ship exploded and killed the remaining Jagaroth, igniting the primordial soup that sparked life on Earth. Only Scaroth survived, caught within the warp field during the explosion. Scaroth was splintered across time on Earth in twelve distinct forms, all psychically connected to each other. The various 'splinters' of Scaroth have been working together to advance human technology to the point where the most advanced splinter, Count Scarlioni in the late 20th century, can build a warp field capable of taking Scaroth back in time to undo the event that caused the destruction of the Jagaroth. That it also spells doom for the current inhabitants of Earth is of no consequence.

In her true form, Scarlett is a green-skinned humanoid with a single Cyclopean eye in the centre of her head. Her mossy skin resembles small tendrils, leading some who see her true face to erroneously describe her as a one-eyed octopus. Using a Raxacoricofallapatorian device that one of Scaroth's previous splinters acquired and adapted, Scarlett killed a Parisian prostitute and took her skin. By wearing it, Scarlett is able to transfer sustenance and keep it appearing youthful and healthy.

In her human form Scarlett is charming and cunning. She keeps her body in peak physical condition and has adapted the Raxacoricfallapatorian voice modulator to enhance her voice; her tone is silky and sultry. She uses her reputation as a diva to hide her occasional psychic 'meetings' with her splinter selves; she is known to storm out of meetings, rehearsals, and even performances when this happens. Understanding that such behaviour could cause troubles even for an international sensation,

SCARLETT VALENTIN

AWARENESS	3	PRESENCE	5
COORDINATION	3	RESOLVE	4
INGENUITY	5	STRENGTH	3

SKILLS

Athletics 4, Convince 4, Craft 3, Fighting 3, Knowledge 6, Marksman 2, Science 5, Subterfuge 4, Survival 3, Technology 5, Transport 3.

TRAITS

Alien
Alien Appearance (Major): Without a skin suit, Scarlett is utterly inhuman.
Arrogant
Attractive: +2 bonus to any rolls that involve Scarlett's looks. She loses this bonus if she removes her mask.
Boffin: Scarlett can create Gadgets.
Charming: +2 bonus to attempts to use charm.
Dark Secret (Minor): Actually an alien.
Indomitable
Last of my Kind: -2 to any but life threatening rolls when alone.
Obsession (Major): Save the Jagaroth!
Screamer! Spend a Story Point to stun anything or anyone else in the room for one action.
Special – Splintered: Scarlett is in contact with her other splinters, granting her a wide selection of knowledge and experience. It also distracts her on occasion. Whenever Scarlett is encountered, roll two dice. If the dice come up doubles then Scarlett is effectively Stunned for several seconds as she communes with her other selves.
Time Traveller (Major): Due the knowledge gained from her splintered form, Scarlett is familiar with all Tech Levels prior to her own.
Voice of Authority: +2 bonus to Presence and Convince rolls.
Wealthy: Thanks to her predecessors, Scarlett is never in need of money for personal use, although her aggressive support of emerging technologies makes new acquisitions and contacts important for her.

EQUIPMENT

Adaptive Skin Suit (Major Gadget; Shapeshift, Restriction: Limited to preserved skin; 2 Story Points)
Micromeson Scanner (Minor Gadget, Scan, 1 Story Point)

TECH LEVEL: 7 STORY POINTS: 6

Scarlett has taken to using a psychic-dampening drug for critical performances. This is starting to spark rumours of terrestrial drug use.

As with Scaroth's other splinters, Scarlett's primary motivation is to accelerate the advancement of new technologies in order to achieve the goal of time travel. She has also heard rumours of other aliens in London who may already have access to such technologies and uses her charm and cunning to find them. Scarlett is not opposed to allying herself with other aliens such as Napoleon so long as their goals align and, in the end, Scarlett maintains the upper hand. If she is successful, then she will sing one last song to herald the end of a world that never existed.

ANTOINE PETIT

Antoine Petit is Scarlett's long-suffering manager and handler. Prior to meeting Scarlett, Antoine was the owner of a small Parisian theatre. He took a chance on the then-unknown Scarlett, who had seemingly appeared out of nowhere but had a beautiful countenance and a voice to match. Her performances were more successful than Antoine could have ever imagined and, as Scarlett's star rose, she asked him to remain with her as her manager. Antoine eagerly agreed and has toured the world with his enigmatic ingénue who often acts as if she's the boss.

ANTOINE PETIT

AWARENESS	2	PRESENCE	4
COORDINATION	2	RESOLVE	3
INGENUITY	2	STRENGTH	2

SKILLS
Convince 3, Craft 3 (Theatre Director 5), Knowledge 3 (Arts 5).

TRAITS
Cowardly (Minor Bad): -2 penalty to any fear roll.
Unadventurous (Major Bad): Petit avoids adventure and excitement.

TECH LEVEL: 4 STORY POINTS: 3

Antoine is a small man with a timid personality; only Scarlett's continued success and the increasing amount of money in his pockets fosters any sort of backbone. He is infatuated with Scarlett but lacks the self-confidence to pursue more than a professional relationship with her; he is jealous of those who are able to successfully gain her attention. He knows that there is something 'off' about her and suspects that she isn't who she claims to be. In spite of that, Antoine decided early on that he wouldn't ask too many questions; people who came to his Parisian theatre claiming to know Scarlett, often from the gutters of Parisian society, tended to disappear.

ROLLO FORD

Celebrities like Scarlett Valentin are always in need of protection, and currently that comes in the form of Rollo Ford, a bare-knuckle fighter and former sailor who acts as her bodyguard and manservant. Rollo is an intimidating figure, slightly shorter than average but stout and well-muscled, with an assortment of tattoos all over his body. His head is shaven but he usually covers it with his red felt bowler. In spite of his brutish appearance Rollo is quite bright and has a wealth of knowledge gleaned from life on the high seas and the many ports he's visited.

ROLLO FORD

AWARENESS	4	PRESENCE	4
COORDINATION	3	RESOLVE	4
INGENUITY	3	STRENGTH	5

SKILLS
Athletics 3, Convince 3 (Intimidate 5), Fighting 4, Knowledge 2, Marksman 2, Transport 2.

TRAITS
Brave: Rollo is brave and gets a+2 bonus to any Resolve roll when her needs to show courage.
Distinctive (Minor Bad): Rollo's imposing form and numerous tattoos garner him a -2 penalty to rolls to blend in. Others have a +2 bonus to remember or recognise Rollo if they've seen him before or heard about him.
Quick Reflexes: Rollo always goes first in his action round unless taken by surprise.
Tough: Rollo reduces total damage taken by 2.
Unattractive: Rollo takes a -2 penalty to any rolls that involve his looks and he gets a +2 to intimidate rolls.

TECH LEVEL: 4 STORY POINTS: 3

Rollo is unaware of Scarlett's true nature and her sometimes questionable activities don't bother him; he's seen worse. His job is to protect her and he knows how to keep his mouth shut. Scarlett even relies on him whenever brute force is needed. So long as she pays well and keeps him out of prison, Rollo is content. This nonchalant attitude would, of course, change if he ever saw her true form.

THE TORCHWOOD INSTITUTE

The Torchwood Institute was established in 1879 by Queen Victoria in the aftermath of an attempt on her life at the Torchwood Estate in Scotland involving a werewolf. The monks who worshipped the werewolf, the Brethen, forced Queen Victoria to stop at the Torchwood Estate by blocking the railway and forcing the owner, Sir Robert MacLeish, to help them expose the Queen to the werewolf's bite so she would herself become one.

The plot was foiled by both the timely arrival of the Doctor and Rose, as well as Sir Robert's late father George. George had been a friend of Prince Albert and together they'd designed the observatory as a trap to destroy the werewolf, combining the Koh-i-Noor diamond and the telescope into a deadly 'light chamber'. The Doctor was able to spring the trap, but Sir Robert was killed by the werewolf in the process.

While the Doctor helped foil the plan, Queen Victoria felt that both the Doctor and aliens in general were enemies of the British Empire (although she knighted the Doctor and Rose before banishing them). She made the Torchwood Estate the headquarters of a new organisation designed to protect the British Empire from such threats and appointed the newly widowed Lady Isobel MacLeish as its head. While her home remains the centre of the Torchwood Institute's operations, Lady Isobel travels the empire and spends most of her time in London where alien activity seems most concentrated.

Less than two decades old, Torchwood is still finding its feet. It's not yet the powerhouse that it will grow into in the next century, but its agents have an almost unlimited authority to operate as they see fit. Torchwood also has access to alien technology that they are putting to use in the field. For the Paternoster Gang, Torchwood is often a rival that can come in and shut down their investigations at any time.

While the aliens of the Paternoster Gang are technically under Torchwood's jurisdiction, Lady Isobel keeps them at arm's length for several reasons. The Paternoster Gang is often good at ferreting out problems that the Torchwood Institute misses (and unveiling alien technology that Torchwood can hoard) and they are constant magnets for the Doctor.

LADY ISOBEL MACLEISH

Lady Isobel MacLeish is the Director of the Torchwood Institute, although she prefers to use her noble title in polite company. Since losing her husband to a Werewolf and being appointed to track down similar menaces, Lady Isobel has thrown herself into her work, feeling that she is honouring her husband's memory with each new alien threat she helps neutralise.

LADY ISOBEL MACLEISH

AWARENESS	3	PRESENCE	4
COORDINATION	3	RESOLVE	5
INGENUITY	3	STRENGTH	3

SKILLS
Athletics 2, Convince 3, Craft 3, Fighting 2, Knowledge 4, Marksman 3, Subterfuge 3, Survival 3, Technology 3.

TRAITS
Brave: Lady Isobel has personally faced down aliens. She gets a +2 bonus to any Resolve roll when she needs to show her courage.
Charming: As the leader of the Torchwood Institute, Lady Isobel has learned how to manipulate people. She gets a +2 bonus on charm attempts.
Empathic: Lady Isobel can read people fairly well. She gets a +2 bonus when empathising or reading another person.
Friends (Major): Lady Isobel has friends at the highest levels, up to and including the Queen.
Obligation (Major): Lady Isobel 'is' the Torchwood Institute.
Noble: Lady Isobel is a gentlewoman and gets a +2 bonus on social rolls against commoners.
Psychic Training: As with all Torchwood agents, Lady Isobel has a degree of mental conditioning that makes it difficult to control her. She gets a +2 bonus to Resolve rolls when trying to resist psychic attack or deception.
Unlucky: In spite of her prestige, Lady Isobel suffers more than her share of tragedies. Fate will likely not be kind to her.

TECH LEVEL: 4 STORY POINTS: 9

Unlike the Queen, Lady Isobel harbours no ill will towards the Doctor and only reluctantly pursues him; her feelings are why Madame Vastra and the Paternoster Gang are left largely unmolested, providing that they don't interfere with Torchwood business. When encountered, Lady Isobel is warm and friendly, preferring to chat about differences over tea than arguing. When crossed, however, Lady Isobel has a fiery spirit and a determination to win at all costs. She asserts her authority and pulls out all stops to maintain it.

SIR EDWARD TOLLIVER

Sir Edward Tolliver is, for lack of a better term, a thief. While a fairly accomplished engineer himself, Edward has always lacked inspiration and has difficulty moving beyond merely improving existing designs. He was recruited by Torchwood and knighted for his work in creating an analytical engine, although the true credit for that should have gone to Charles Babbage and his son Major General Henry Prevost Babbage. Edward corresponded with Henry and learned the inner workings of both the difference and analytical engine from him. Having gleaned their secrets, Edward built his own 'Tolliver engine' which the Torchwood Institute now uses.

Edward's deception did not fool Lady Isobel, but she appreciated his tenacity and, in the absence of being able to recruit someone like Professor Barlow, Torchwood would settle for someone who had the ability to tap the abilities of others and 'borrow' their designs. Thus far Edward has performed this task admirably, although he rightly fears the day in which a true mechanical genius is recruited and Edward would be made redundant. It may even be worth killing over...

SIR EDWARD TOLLIVER

AWARENESS	3	PRESENCE	5
COORDINATION	2	RESOLVE	4
INGENUITY	4	STRENGTH	2

SKILLS

Convince 4, Craft 3, Fighting 3 (Fencing 5), Knowledge 4, Marksman 2, Medicine 2, Science 3, Subterfuge 4, Technology 4, Transport 4.

TRAITS

Charming: Edward is quite charming and makes friends easily. He gets a +2 bonus to attempts to use charm.
Noble: Edward is a knight and gets a +2 in social situations against commoners.
Obligation (Major): Edward is always at the beck and call of the Torchwood Institute.
Obsession (Major): Edward is consumed with proving his worth and, ironically, this includes stealing others' work to pass off as his own.
Photographic Memory: Edward forgets nothing. If he even glances at a blueprint he can memorise all of the particulars.
Psychic Training: Edward is trained to resist psychic influence and gains a +2 bonus to Resolve rolls when trying to resist psychic attack or deception.
Uncreative: Edward has difficulty thinking outside the box. He takes a -2 to any Technology roll when trying to fix a faulty device or create a new design.

TECH LEVEL: 4 STORY POINTS: 3

ALLAN QUINCY RIDDELL

Allan Quincy Riddell is less full Torchwood operative and more of a contractor; as a big game hunter he prefers stalking his prey across the African savannah or through the Bengalese rainforests than the rookeries of London. That said, Allan is not only an invaluable asset to Torchwood when they need to hunt alien technology in the more remote areas of the world, but he is equally capable of hunting, capturing and, when necessary, killing dangerous aliens and their minions in the back alleys and sewers of London.

Allan is good at what he does and he knows it; he always takes the time to try to impress any ladies present with the stories of his exploits (Rhona barely endures it). Allan also has a tendency to 'forget' that his prey is intelligent. He prefers to see them as exotic beasts and trophies. This arrogance makes him difficult to control when discretion is called for, and Allan tends to see the brokering of negotiations as little more than setting a trap to neutralise an alien while their defences are down.

ALLAN RIDDELL

AWARENESS	4	PRESENCE	4
COORDINATION	5	RESOLVE	4
INGENUITY	3	STRENGTH	4

SKILLS

Athletics 4, Craft (Traps) 4, Fighting 5, Knowledge 2, Marksman 5, Medicine 2, Subterfuge 3, Survival 4.

TRAITS

Arrogant: Allan believes his own hype. His arrogance and bravery give him a +2 to resist fear and hopelessness, but he suffers a -1 to social interactions with those whom he feels are ignorant or inferior.
Charming: Allan can certainly sway opinions and there is a mystique about his lifestyle. He gets a +2 bonus whenever trying to charm his way through an encounter.
Keen Senses (Major): Allan has sharpened all of his senses; he gets a +2 bonus in any instance when using Awareness to notice or spot something.
Psychic Training: Allan is trained to resist psychic influence and gains a +2 bonus to Resolve rolls when trying to resist psychic attack or deception.
Quick Reflexes: Allan usually goes first in a given round.
Resourceful Pockets: As a big game and alien hunter, Allan usually has useful things in his pockets. He can spend a Story Point or try to roll a double when he needs something specific.
Run for Your Life! Allan has a lot of practice running from injured, angry creatures. He gets a +1 bonus to his speed when fleeing.
Sense of Direction: Allan gets a +2 bonus on rolls when trying to regain direction or get from point A to B.
Tough: Allan is made of stern stuff. He reduces the amount of damage he takes by 2.

TECH LEVEL: 4 STORY POINTS: 3

It is precisely because of Allan's singular perspective that Lady Isobel prefers to keep him at arm's length, giving her plausible deniability if Allan's methods go a bit too far or cause too much collateral damage.

One thing that works in Allan's favour is that he is a bona fide hero. His exploits in Africa and Asia are well-documented and inspired aspiring writer H Rider Haggard, with whom Allan struck up a friendship. In fact, Haggard actually wrote about Allan's first major expedition for Torchwood under the title of *King Solomon's Mines*. Lady Isobel managed to stop the publication of the original manuscript and Haggard extensively re-wrote it, but rumours exist of original copies that contain sensitive (or at least embarrassing) information about the expedition. It is an open secret amongst the public that 'Allan Quatermain' is a thinly veiled Allan Quincy Riddell.

RHONA AUSTEN

This Torchwood recruit is an enigma to Madame Vastra, as she bears an uncanny resemblance to Clara Oswald, who splintered into several separate lives when she entered the Doctor's own timestream. Rhona is especially alarming to Vastra in that she apparently shared the Earth with another version of Clara that died when the Doctor and the Paternoster Gang fought the Great Intelligence. Has Rhona already fulfilled her mission and helped the Doctor, or is she still preparing to do so? Or is Rhona someone – or something – else entirely?

Thus far only one thing is certain – Rhona is human, or at least that's what Strax's scans have shown. As far as Vastra can tell from her few meetings with Lady Isobel, the Director of Torchwood is unaware of the resemblance, although Vastra can't rule out that Rhona is being used as bait for the Doctor. What is known is that Rhona is an experienced Torchwood operative, having worked in Edinburgh and Glasgow before being transferred to London. Rhona herself seems unaware of her condition, or at least she has not revealed anything to the Paternosters.

Rhona also exudes the confidence, and sometimes recklessness, of her doppelganger. She assumes that she is going to succeed, and usually does. She is one of Torchwood's most effective agents. Unlike Allan, Rhona prefers to use wit and guile to capture aliens or procure their technology and she is perfectly willing to work with the Paternoster Gang so long as their goals coincide.

RHONA AUSTEN

AWARENESS	3	PRESENCE	3
COORDINATION	3	RESOLVE	4
INGENUITY	4	STRENGTH	2

SKILLS

Athletics 3, Convince 4, Fighting 3 (Stick-umbrella 5), Knowledge 4, Marksman 4, Medicine 1, Science 3, Subterfuge 4, Survival 3, Technology 3, Transport 3.

TRAITS

Attractive: Rhona is quite attractive and gets a +2 bonus to any rolls that involve her looks.
Brave: Rhona gets a +2 bonus to any Resolve roll when she needs to show courage.
Eccentric (Minor Bad): Rhona prefers to be in control at all times, much to the chagrin of her partners.
Impulsive: Rhona is overconfident and sometimes doesn't think things through before acting.
Insatiable Curiosity: She will investigate anything that sparks her curiosity unless she first passes a Resolve + Ingenuity roll at -2.
Lucky: Rhona may re-roll any 'double 1s'.
Obligation (Major): Rhona is a loyal agent of the Torchwood Institute.
Psychic Training: Rhona is trained to resist psychic influence and gains a +2 bonus to Resolve rolls when trying to resist psychic attack or deception.

TECH LEVEL: 4 STORY POINTS: 3

DR KARFELOV, THE BORAD AND THE LOCH NESS MONSTER

The Doctor has offered two alternative explanations for the sightings of 'Old Nessie' over the centuries, but that's not because he was guessing; the two explanations aren't mutually exclusive. The first is that a Zygon vessel crashed into Loch Ness centuries ago and that the Zygons' 'pet' and source of nourishment, the Apatosaurus-resembling Skarasen (see **The Fourth Doctor Sourcebook**) was mistaken for a prehistoric creature. The second is that the Borad, a disfigured alien scientist from the future, was thrown back to 13th century Earth via a time corridor and also became the source of the legend, as his body was fused with that of a reptilian Morlox that was native to his home world of Karfel.

In truth, the Borad arrived first; his horrific appearance also increased his lifespan (and Karfellians are naturally a bit longer-lived than Earth humans) and he was forced to hide and scavenge while trying to recreate the tools he needed to recreate his old experiments. He learned enough to give the local Scots successful advice when the Black Plague reached Scotland in the following century and this, in spite of his appearance, endeared him enough to the locals for him to become a Scottish Laird and build a home on the shores of Loch Ness, where he could better continue his experiments.

When the Zygon ship came crashing to Earth sometime later, the ship's scanners identified the Borad's bio-chemical experiments as compatible with its own technology and it crash-landed a few miles away in Devil's Punchbowl. Zygon leader Broton made contact with the Borad and struck a deal to ensure the survival of his crew. The Zygons would largely remain in cryogenic storage while the Skarasen grew from an embryo to an animal large enough to feed them, while the Borad ensured their survival. In return, the Zygons offered to share some of their bio-technology with the Borad. It was a deal the Borad quickly accepted.

With the Borad holding most of the cards, it didn't take too long for him to take advantage of his position. It took a couple centuries, but he absorbed and adapted enough Zygon technology to replicate what he needed and then tried to sabotage the Zygon vessel. Unfortunately for him, the Zygons weren't as inactive as they'd claimed and sent the Skarasen to destroy him. The Borad got away but his castle was destroyed. Believing him gone the Zygons went back into torpor, while the Borad rebuilt his estate. Recently, he's reinvented himself as Dr Boris Karfelov, pretending that the resources he'd acquired over the centuries actually came from Russia. He claims to have fled his homeland as a refugee from autocratic rule. He settled in London, sharing his scientific insights and knowledge while opening health clinics throughout the poorer areas. He is considered quite the philanthropist and was even knighted a few years ago by Queen Victoria. He currently teaches at the University of London and has purchased land on Foulness Island to build a manor 'suitable for his station.'

In truth, 'Dr Karfelov' is an imperfect clone – the Borad's true form has a larger, more powerful brain and a human-sized one would not be able to hold all of the knowledge that he has in his hybrid form. Having lived openly amongst humans for so long Dr Karfelov is becoming more like them – he is starting to see himself as something other than a clone, although he still swears loyalty to his 'older brother.' While the Borad schemes to retake Karfel with an army of Tripods, Dr Karfelov is content to live, and even die, as a philanthropic professor.

THE BORAD

The Borad is an alien exile from the planet Karfel. He was a brilliant scientist, Megalen, who took over his planet's government after the Doctor exposed his dangerous experiments. This resulted in an accident where Megalen's body was fused with that of a Morlox, a reptile native to Karfel. Calling himself 'the Borad', he planned to convert the population into creatures like himself.

The Borad was subsequently defeated by the Doctor (with the help of a young HG Wells) and he escaped through the Timelash, a Time Corridor that the Doctor overloaded and left the Borad trapped in AD1179 near Inverness, Scotland. The Borad would have died there were it not for the timely arrival of a damaged Zygon ship, with whom he offered an exchange of services. This enabled the Borad to continue his experiments, including the cloning of himself to become effectively immortal. Unfortunately for the Borad, his cloning experiments revealed that his Morloxian side had become such a part of him that trying to clone a 'human' version of himself led only to imperfect copies. He was stuck in his fused form, although he can 'camouflage' it with Zygon technology. The Borad rarely bothers though, as he is more comfortable in his fused form when lurking about at his manor. He does maintain an imperfect clone, Dr Karfelov, who acts as his 'public face' when necessary.

While he's come to accept life on Earth, the Borad still wants to create a planet of fused creatures like himself. His attempts to create Morloxes on Earth has failed, largely because he can't isolate a 'pure' strain of Morlox genetic material that will thrive on Earth – it needs Karfel's environment to survive. Thus, the Borad wishes to return to his home planet, if not necessarily his own time, to complete his plans, and working with the Napoleon of Crime seems to be the best way to go about it.

CLONE (NEW TRAIT)

Clone is a Special Good Trait costing 3 Character Points and 1 Story Points. The character has a clone; a perfect physical copy of themselves stored securely. If they ever die, the clone will be automatically activated and take their place. In order to make sure the clone knows everything they know, they must regularly visit the storage facility to update the clone's memory engrams (say, between each adventure). If they don't, then when the clone is activated, it will only have memories up to the last update.

Effect: The character literally has another life, which has the attributes, skills, traits and memories of whenever it was last updated.

THE BORAD

AWARENESS	5	PRESENCE	5
COORDINATION	2	RESOLVE	6
INGENUITY	6	STRENGTH	5

SKILLS
Athletics 3, Convince 3, Fighting 4, Knowledge 6, Marksman 2, Medicine 7, Science 7, Subterfuge 4, Survival 3, Technology 4.

TRAITS
Alien
Alien Appearance
Arrogant: The Borad considers himself above those around him. He gains a +2 to resist fear but takes a -1 to social rolls involving anyone he considers inferior to him.
Biochemical Genius: The Borad is considered to have Areas of Expertise for the Science skill in Biology and Chemistry and may create biological or chemical 'Gadgets' using the Jiggery-Pokery rules, substituting Science for Technology when making such gadgets.
Special – Clone: The Borad can create full clones of himself as well as imperfect human clones.

Fast Healing (Major): Attribute Points lost due to injury are regained at 1 point per hour.
Technically Adept: The Borad gets +2 to any Technology roll to fix a broken or faulty device.
Time Traveller (Minor): Tech Level 4.

EQUIPMENT: Laser Pistol L (4/L/L)

TECH LEVEL: 6 STORY POINTS: 9

DR KARFELOV

Dr Karfelov is the latest in a series of clones that is used by the Borad to maintain as a cover and to interact with those with whom the Borad has a relationship. A similar succession of clones, the latest being Laird Boran of Caerfall (an estate near Loch Ness), oversees the Scottish property that the Borad has owned for centuries. Dr Karfelov, on the other hand, is a recent clone who pretends to hail from Russia, fleeing Tsarist rule, and has been granted asylum and a title befitting his station.

Karfelov has the basic personality and some of the memories of the Borad, although his human brain can only hold so much. While highly intelligent, Karfelov lacks the brilliance of his creator and, although he is a highly skilled physician, Karfelov is not a bio-genetic boffin like the Borad. When Karfelov finds his own skills lacking, he calls on his master at Foulness Island for answers.

DR KARFELOV

AWARENESS	3	PRESENCE	4
COORDINATION	3	RESOLVE	4
INGENUITY	5	STRENGTH	2

SKILLS

Convince 4, Knowledge 4, Medicine 5, Science 5, Subterfuge 2, Technology 2.

TRAITS

Charming: Karfelov is designed to blend into society and can be quite charming. He gains a +2 on attempts to use charm.

Distinctive: Karfelov's Russian accent and mannerisms mark him as easily recognisable (unlike his master, Karfelov sports a healthy beard).

Enslaved: Karfelov is conditioned to follow the orders of the Borad and suffers a -2 to attempts to voice opinions contrary to the Borad's wishes.

Noble (Minor): Karfelov is considered to be a country squire.

Time Traveller (Minor): Tech Level 4.

TECH LEVEL: 6 STORY POINTS: 6

JOSEPHINE

Napoleon has been alone without Dalek fellowship for decades and he wants the Borad to rectify the problem. After many attempts, the Borad has finally succeeded in creating a mutant creature that is almost exactly like a Dalek with a casing to match. The Borad has named her Josephine in honour of the real Napoleon's first wife and true love.

Josephine's casing is a combination of spare parts that Napoleon has salvaged from the wreckage of Maxtible House in Chelsea. The result is a bulkier, but still recognisably Dalek design, complete with a rudimentary hovering capability (although the bottom of Josephine's 'skirt' also includes wheels). The Borad has dubbed the new cyborg a 'Steelclad.'

Josephine was an upper class woman before her conversion, named Lyssa Marden. The Borad arranged a carriage accident that killed her parents and pretended to rescue her from death.

While she has been conditioned to accept her new form and to serve both the Borad and Napoleon (the Borad ensured that her loyalty to him takes precedence should Napoleon ever turn against him), some of that nobility remains. Given the Borad's aversion to mirrors Josephine has never actually seen herself and the shock of what she's become could turn her against him.

JOSEPHINE

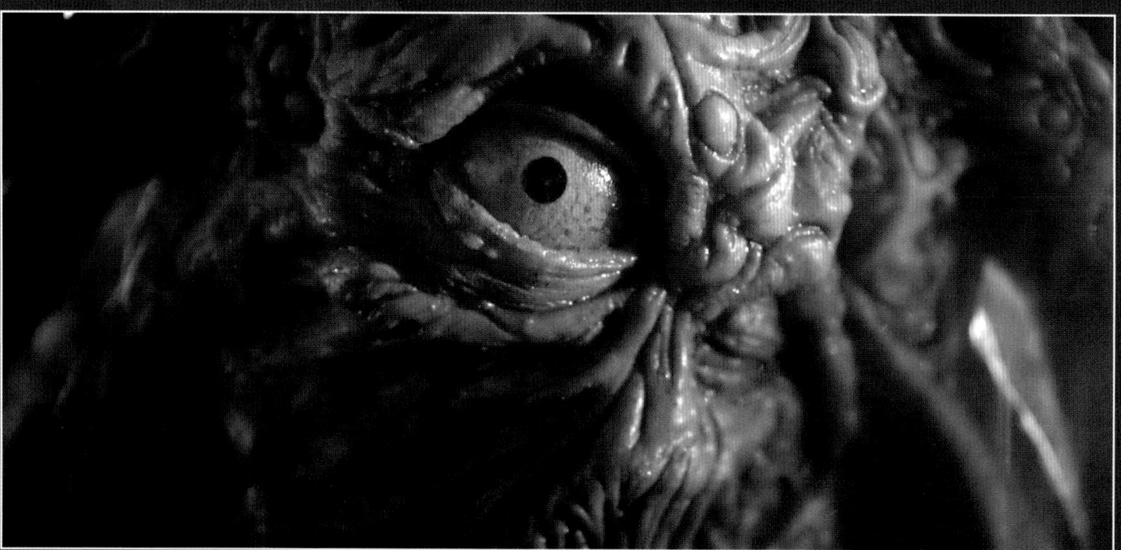

AWARENESS	2	PRESENCE	3
COORDINATION	2	RESOLVE	4
INGENUITY	2	STRENGTH	7*

SKILLS
Convince 2, Fighting 1, Knowledge 3, Marksman 2, Survival 1.

TRAITS
Armour (Minor): Josephine's casing has reinforced armour plating. Reduce damage by 5.
Cyborg: While technically a creature operating a vehicle, Josephine isn't very effective outside of her casing.
Enslaved: Josephine is conditioned to serve the Borad and Napoleon (and in that order).
Environmental (Major): The slight forcefield around Josephine's casing enables her to endure hostile environments.
Fear Factor (3): While most Victorians don't understand what she is, Josephine can frighten them with just a few words. She gets a +6 to rolls when trying to intimidate or terrify others.
Flight (Minor): Josephine can hover at Speed 1, but she can do little more than climb steps with it, as she is only capable of hovering a few feet.
Natural Weapon – Claw: Joesphine's manipulator ends in a three-fingered claw that is capable of doing +2 damage.
Natural Weapon – Flamethrower: Josephine is equipped with a flamethrower that does 7 (3/7/10) damage to a 5-foot radius. Characters hit by the flames also catch fire – until such fires are extinguished (the Gamesmaster determines the difficulty), burning characters take 4 damage each round.
Voice of Authority: Josephine is used to barking orders as a noble and gets a +2 bonus to Presence and Convince rolls when ordering people to do things for her.

*The mutant inside has different Attributes when removed from the Steelclad casing. Movement outside of the armour is incredibly limited (Speed 1) and they do not usually survive very long. If the mutant is exposed at any time, damage inflicted to Josephine may bypass the armour.

AWARENESS	2	PRESENCE	2
COORDINATION	1	RESOLVE	4
INGENUITY	2	STRENGTH	5

SKILLS: As above.

TRAITS: **Alien Appearance, Climbing (Minor), Fear Factor (4), Immunity (Radiation), Natural Weapons – Tentacles (2/5/7), Slow (Minor), Voice of Authority**

TECH LEVEL: 4 STORY POINTS: 3

VICTORIAN ADVENTURERS

VICTORIAN ADVENTURERS

Now you know something of the world the Paternosters inhabit, it is time we looked at creating the characters that are a part of it. Your heroes, who will stand ready to defend London from a host of strange creatures and mysterious plans.

YOUR OWN PATERNOSTER GANG

Before you begin to create individual characters, you all need to discuss together what sort of a group you are going to play. Will you be gentleman adventurers, scientific investigators or East-end criminals? Your characters will need to be able to find some connection, even if they are to be strangers when the campaign begins. This is also useful for the Gamemaster who needs to know the sort of campaign you all want to play. There is no point in the Gamemaster creating several adventures set at society balls if the players all want to create a gang of smugglers working along the docks on the Thames. The following offer suggestions about the sort of group you might create together.

PATERNOSTER IRREGULARS

Your group might be friends of the Paternoster Gang themselves as part of the Paternoster Irregulars. Anyone might owe the Paternoster Gang a favour, so your characters can come from any walk of life, and find themselves brought together to help the Paternoster Gang solve a particularly tricky or dangerous case. In fact, you may wish to simply play Madame Vastra, Jenny and Strax yourself! This is the default group set-up we assume elsewhere in the book.

GENTLEMAN ADVENTURERS

Your group is wealthy enough to need no occupation and so chases aliens and solve crimes simply to stave off boredom. The characters come from the upper classes, but might also bring trusted servants to help them investigate the strange occurrences that strike their interest. Money is not much of a barrier to their adventures, and they have plenty of time on their hands to follow any trail. However, they must remain discrete as the last thing they want is a scandal.

SCIENTIFIC INVESTIGATORS

For your group, investigations are all about discovery rather than adventure. There are a lot of strange things going on in the city, and some of them might even be alien. Your group is made up of scientists and their assistants, with maybe a few burly former soldiers for back up. Together you seek out new advances and lost alien technology to try and understand the greater secrets of the universe. In some cases the technology isn't quite as lost as previously believed, and its owners might come looking for it.

ALIEN REFUGEES

Earth has a tendency to gather the lost and the strange, and your group is made up of a fair amount of both. You are all aliens; some stranded here, others in hiding. You have gathered together for mutual support and protection. Sadly there are those that would do you harm. The Torchwood Institute constantly hunts for new study subjects and Napoleon is always looking to press-gang aliens to serve in his criminal empire. Your own species might come to hunt you down too. Will you find a place to hide – such as in Leper Hall – or find a way to strike back?

CONSULTING DETECTIVES

Like Sherlock Holmes you have chosen to solve crime for a hobby. Where the police have failed, you offer your services to investigate interesting problems brought to your door. You need not all be detectives, as such an operation will need plenty of support. Several different expert opinions might be needed to understand the stranger clues.

CRIMINAL GANG

Whether human or alien, everyone has to make a living. You have few of the advantages of birth and turned to less than legal means to make ends meet. Together, your group has a base in one of the less salubrious areas of the city, where you build your own criminal empire. To do so you will undoubtedly come to blows with other more ruthless criminals who seek the same goals. But you need not be the worst kind of people. You might choose to use what money you make to help out the more desperate in your community. You may even take on jobs to right a wrong or do something that the police cannot, rather than to turn a profit.

BUSINESS ENTREPRENEURS

Your group is on the look out for new business opportunities. With strange creatures and new technology for the taking, there is plenty of potential for profit. The black market for alien goods can be very exotic – and very dangerous. Several different skills will be required to protect your investments too.

CREATING PATERNOSTER CHARACTERS

Now you know a little more about the shape and style of the game you all want to play, we can start looking at creating individual characters. The process is

DEFYING EXPECTATIONS

The Doctor's companions are all exceptional individuals, defying societal norms and expectations. They are exceptions to their class, their gender, even their species – and so should your characters be too! When creating your own characters, don't let historical accuracy get in the way of a good concept, and don't get overly drawn into making sure all the details are right. What's more important is creating a fun, exciting character to accompany the Doctor – or the Paternoster Gang – on adventures in Victorian London!

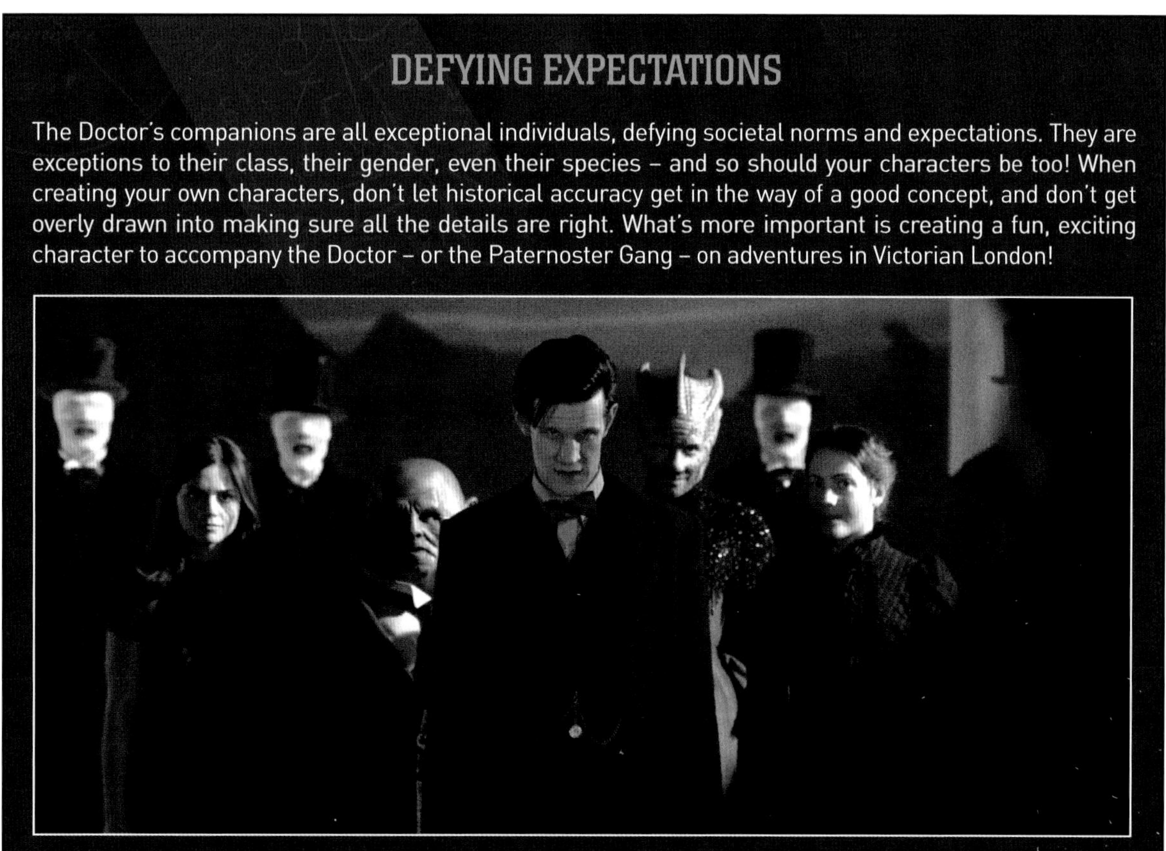

exactly the same as described in the **Doctor Who Roleplaying Game Core Rulebook**, but in this chapter we'll offer a few extra things you may wish to consider along with a few new traits and abilities.

To give you a few ideas to start with, we offer a few general archetypes of the sort of character you might play. We've divided them by social class for convenience, but that should not limit any aspect of your character.

For instance, only the wealthy have the money and recreational time to pursue a career in science; but many of the middle classes can raise the funds; and a lower class lab assistant might learn more than their superiors if they pay attention. The reverse is also true, where a lower class character might be forced into a life of crime, a gentleman might become a thief for the adventure of it all.

UPPER CLASS ARCHETYPES

Noble characters are used to a life of privilege, but also one of boredom. As it is seen as beneath them to earn a living, they often follow a hobby as others might a career. For the gentlemen, eldest sons are brought up to inherit, while younger sons join the military or the church (although the latter has become more middle class with little land income from a parsonage). Daughters are expected to learn exceptional manners and marry well for the sake of the family if not for themselves.

Philanthropist

You are keenly aware of the advantages you have had in life. Feeling that it is a duty to minister to the less fortunate, you spend your time doing charity work. You might have become an advocate for social change, speaking at meetings and acting as a patron or fundraiser for social projects. However you might also take further steps, going out to help the poor directly, bringing food and supplies to the needy.

Academic

You have chosen to spend your time studying, having found whole worlds in the books that surround you. You spent your days in the family library and begged your parents to provide a tutor when the library was exhausted. You have amassed a great deal of knowledge, but mainly for the joy of learning rather than any particular purpose. Soon you will find your expertise of great use to some strange new friends.

Scientist

You have discovered the beauty of knowledge, but reading alone is not enough for you. You are part of the vanguard of new scientists looking to push the boundaries of human knowledge further. You have your own laboratory and spend your days engrossed in a series of experiments. In this way you hope to unlock the secrets of the universe.

Army Officer

While anyone might enlist, officers usually come from the upper classes as a commission can be purchased. Your family see nothing wrong with this, believing the wealthy have an innate understanding of how to lead. You have served across the British Empire, in foreign climes all around the globe. Now, returning to London, you find the strange diversity of Earth is far greater than you ever expected.

Politician
While many new politicians are getting into government through the middle classes, the country is still run by the nobility. Only the wealthy have the time to mount a campaign and attend to the affairs of their office. The House of Lords still controls what becomes law. You might want to maintain the status quo or, following the calls for social change, stand on the vanguard of reform. The strangest people have brought their problems to you looking for your help; it seems the world is changing faster than you expected.

MIDDLE CLASS ARCHETYPES

The middle class is the professional class. It is made up of working entrepreneurs, educated white collar workers and business owners. The middle classes are on the rise, which makes the upper class very nervous indeed. Characters from this class tend to be full of hope that they can carve out a new life in this incredible age.

Professional
The Empire requires an army of bureaucrats to keep it running. Clerks of all forms labour daily to keep the government and the businesses of Britain ticking along. You have joined their ranks in the hopes of moving up the nascent corporate ladder. However, with university training you might also become a doctor or a lawyer, where you might make an entrance into higher society with the right contacts.

Factory Owner
Whether you inherited it or built it with your own toil, you run one of the powerhouses of the industrial revolution. From your office you look out on a domain of steam-driven production. There is a never ending supply of people looking for work. But sometimes you wonder if you should allow your employees the rights some of the rabble rousers shout about in the market places. As long as they keep the machines running it's all the same to you. You pay little attention to the workers, especially as sometimes not all of them seem human...

Investor
This is an age of opportunity, and you have chosen to grasp it with both hands. You are always looking for the next investment, be it cutting-edge science, a new novelist or simply a shopkeeper with a knack for business. You have set up several new businesses, all for a cut of the profits of course. But you are always keeping an ear to the ground for the next big thing. Each day brings some new gadget or mystery to the public eye. The trick is to catch it before anyone else. You have an eye on a few things, but some of them defy understanding, and others don't appear to be of this Earth.

Shopkeeper
You have a small business with a shop on one of London's busier streets. It could sell anything; fresh bread, meat, books, perhaps even a little of everything. The city is full of 'Curiosity Shops' containing all manner of strange and interesting goods. You know plenty of locals, and especially your customers. So you hear plenty of gossip about the local area every day, and some of it sounds very strange indeed.

LOWER CLASS ARCHETYPES

The working classes makes up the great majority of the people of Britain. They all work very long hours for very little pay. Few have any worker's rights but without a job they and their family will likely starve. Crowded into small terraced houses, the lower classes have learned to live close together. A greater sense of community exists here, even if few can afford to share what they have.

Labourer
People will always be needed to lift and carry stuff. You are strong and capable, and find it reasonably easy to find work. The only problem is that you have to know where to look and line up each day hoping they need enough labourers today. Luckily, the docks always need workers, and people often look to move house or goods along the streets.

However, if you are really stuck there are a few jobs available for those who don't ask questions. Strange men need mysterious boxes full of odd equipment taken to some out of the way places. So you do as you are told and keep quiet; you've heard stories about those that don't.

Trader
While you are not a shopkeeper or a businessman, you make a living buying and selling. You might have a barrow or a market stall. You might even carry your wares in your coat and walk the city seeking customers. What you sell changes depending on the deals you can make. You might buy some bread cheaply once it is not longer fresh and hope to sell it before it goes stale. Sometimes you find something on the street that you figure someone might offer a few coins for. As long as the previous owner doesn't come looking for it, all to the good.

Criminal
It is hard to make ends meet in the poorer parts of the city. Even with a well-paying job in a factory or in service, hunger and poverty are never far away. Of course, those already destitute, homeless and jobless have little other option. You need not turn to murder, but theft, pick pocketing and burglary are commonplace. There are always plenty of people who will do business without asking questions, even when you have blood on your hands.

Factory Worker
The city is full of machines. Factories daily belch smoke into the air as steam engines drive acres of machinery day and night. The money is comparatively good for those who find work in a factory, but also dangerous. No one will stop the machines for the mere safety of the workers. Children or those with nimble fingers are sent in to free cogs and jams when production is slowed. Not all of them are quick enough to avoid injury.

Publican/Barmaid
London is littered with public houses and gin palaces. You work the bar or serve the tables in one of the many hostelries. Pubs are community centres as much as places to drink, and all the latest news always finds a way to your ears. People bring their troubles here, or work hard to drink them away. You meet all sorts here, some very strange indeed.

ALIEN CHARACTERS

Strangely, it is not as difficult to play an alien character in Victorian London as it might be in the modern age. The Victorians have got used to seeing strange people, especially in London. All manner of people have come to the city from all the corners of the Earth to seek their fortune. While people from foreign climes are not entirely unusual, they have come to London is this era in far greater number.

A LIFE IN SERVICE

Servants make up a whole separate category of working class archetypes. Service is one of the better jobs a working class person can expect to find, and competition is fierce. Of prime importance is a reference of 'character' from a previous employer, and without one it is almost impossible to find work. There are many promotions to be had in the industry, either within one family's home or by making a sideways move to a larger house for better wages or prestige.

While there are several different jobs and positions for servants, they do break down into two simple rules. The first is that, male or female, the lower your position, the harder and heavier the work. The second is that gender defines much of the work you are expected to do. Men are employed for most of the outside work, such as carrying luggage and escorting the family carriage. Women are employed for most of the indoor work, cleaning and laundry. Interestingly, it is men who are often employed as 'Footmen' to stand around looking pretty. Footmen are often given elaborate livery (uniform) and stand 'on hand' around the house. The more you have standing around doing nothing, the more wealth you must have. At the top of the servant's power structure are the butler and the housekeeper. The butler is the head servant, also trusted with the family silverware. The housekeeper organises the running of the house in terms of cleaning and laundry, under the direction of the lady of the house. In some houses the cook may also have a privileged position, especially if they are very good at what they do. In general, most houses have at least one housemaid to clean and manage the house, more if the house is bigger.

Whole communities have developed in several areas, such as the Jewish quarters of Hoxton and the Chinese community in Limehouse.

This means that anyone who looks a little different to the Victorian is simply assumed to be foreign. Even if you have green skin or look like a potato, that must just be what people are like "where you come from". Of course, antenna or mandibles and an extra pair of arms are trickier to justify. But essentially, any humanoid will simply be treated as a foreigner for the most part.

The other thing that will help an alien avoid notice is their adoption of a class and the right clothing. As long as you 'fit in', people will treat you that way, and be very glad to do so. Madame Vastra dresses like a high-born woman and so is treated that way. The signs of class are a convenient short-hand for how to deal with anything the Victorian finds odd. They might not know how to talk to a green lizard, but they do know how to address a lady of quality. Of course, you do have to be careful not to push your luck. Madame Vastra usually wears a veil to make things a little easier. There are some things people find difficult to ignore. But more often than not the Victorians would rather ignore the strange than pass comment on it. Denial is a powerful ally when faced with the unknown or exotic.

NEW TRAITS

GOOD TRAITS

Agent of Scotland Yard (Minor Good Trait)
You have a few contacts at New Scotland Yard, the new home of the Metropolitan Police, or you do work for them on the side. You may have particular knowledge they have found useful, or perhaps they somehow owe you a favour. Either way, you have a certain degree of access not usually granted to the public.

Effect: You know enough detectives well enough to get inside information on crime in the city. You can investigate active crime scenes and ask for reasonably up to date information on ongoing cases. Quite often, Scotland Yard will come to you to get your thoughts on a baffling case.

Imprinted Memories (Special Good Trait)
You have absorbed the memories of someone else, a whole lifetime's worth in fact. You might have accidentally triggered a Cybermen infostamp, or maintained telepathic contact with someone else's mind for too long. While you have not inherited the personality of the person in question, you can sometimes access their memories. Imprinted Memories is a Special Good Trait that costs 3 Character Points.

Effect: You must construct a rough persona that you have been imbued with the memories of. It might be a Dalek, Time Lord, famous scientist or even Queen Victoria herself. The person in question is either highly skilled or has specialised knowledge you do not have. You may spend a Story Point to trigger one of the following effects for the duration of the scene:

- Access to deeply personal or intimate knowledge that only that person would know. Gain a +2 bonus to rolls where that knowledge might prove beneficial (Gamemaster's discretion).
- Grant you access to a skill you do not have, temporarily granting you a rating of 3 points in a skill you only have at 0.
- Allow you to act as if you are from the persona's Tech Level.

Person of Repute (Major Good Trait)
You are considered a person of good character and standing. Your word is your bond and you have proved to be upright and morally proper at all times. So when the finger of suspicion points in your direction, people have a hard time believing it might possibly be anything to do with you.

Effect: When you are accused of a crime or wrongdoing, you may spend a Story Point. If you do, the accusation falls of deaf ears and you are instantly discounted as a suspect, even if you are found with a bloody knife standing over the victim. People will insist there must be another explanation. Unfortunately, hard evidence and the Gamemaster's decision may overrule this reputation should new information later come to light.

Unthreatening (Major Good Trait)
You are not seen as a threat. In fact, you are automatically assumed not to be a physical threat when the fists or bullets fly. It is common for the Victorians to think this of women, but also the young or the hopelessly academic might be overlooked as well. Whenever combat breaks out, as long as you don't participate, you will be left alone and ignored.

Effect: As long as you haven't acted at the Fighting step of combat, you cannot be targeted by an enemy. As soon as you make an attack or fail to surrender to the victors, this effect ends.

BAD TRAITS

Jingoist (Minor Bad Trait)
You have an unwavering belief in the superiority of the British Empire and her people. It's not that other nations or people are bad, they just cannot be as organised, intelligent or all round amazing as the British and their way of life.

Effect: Your enthusiastic bigotry gives you a -2 penalty when dealing with anyone who is not British (or a loyal subject of the empire).

Know your Place (Major Bad)
Everyone, even the rich, knows that they have a part to play in the machinery of Empire. You are so consumed with this that obedience has become a gut instinct for you.

Effect: When given an order or instruction by a social superior, you will obey without question unless you first spend a Story Point.

Marginalised (Minor Bad Trait)
Due to your gender, ethnic background or even your sexuality, you have to work harder to prove yourself or get your voice heard. You suffer prejudice at every turn, often hearing that certain tasks or positions are considered 'unsuitable' for you simply due to your background.

Effect: You suffer a -2 penalty when dealing with anyone on a professional basis as what you consider work, everyone else seems to think is simply your hobby.

Persistent Illness (Minor/Major Bad Trait)
Some time ago, perhaps as a child, you suffered a terrible illness. It nearly killed you, but you somehow survived; it has, however, permanently damaged you in such a way medical science and natural healing can never repair. Alternatively, you might be still caught in the grip of a disease that will eventually kill you, but will allow you a few years of health before it finally takes you.

Effect: You are often debilitated by your illness, perhaps wracked with a cough that leaves blood on your handkerchief, or suddenly overcome with pain. As a Minor Bad Trait, your illness occurs every time you roll a double 1 on a dice roll; you automatically fail the action and are unable to do anything but cough or groan for another D6 rounds. As a Major Bad Trait the bouts of illness are no more severe, but occur when you roll any double on a dice roll (not including additional dice added for Story Points).

Upper Class/Middle Class/Lower Class (Minor Bad Trait)
Each class does things in a slightly different way. The upper class have their balls and the lower class their 'knees ups'. Knowing which fork to use or how not to look the local gangster in the eye are both forms of etiquette. However, if you are used to one and not the other you will run into problems.

Effect: When you are interacting with someone from a different social class, you apply a -4 penalty to the roll. This represents the differences the classes have about how things should be done. Should you fail a roll, the consequences will depend on the company you are keeping. A lower class character failing an etiquette roll in the company of their betters will be thrown out for rudeness, while an upper class character failing a roll to garner information from their inferiors might only find stony silence.

EXISTING TRAITS

There are several traits in the **Doctor Who Roleplaying Game Core Rulebook** that are especially suited for a Paternoster campaign.

GOOD TRAITS

Arrogant – A common trait among the upper classes.
Boffin – Vital for the keen inventor or mad scientist.
Brave – Perfect for the dauntless Victorian explorer.
Face in the Crowd – Useful for servants who fade professionally into the background.
Hypnosis – Mesmerism is a popular entertainment, and a useful trick for a fake psychic.
Indomitable – Just like the British Empire! Huzzah!
Noble – A common but not essential trait for the upper class.
Tough – To survive the streets of old London town.
Voice of Authority – For those who expect to be obeyed.

BAD TRAITS

By the Book – Society is full of protocols.
Code of Conduct – Essential for any gentleman.
Dark Secret – Everything is kept behind closed doors.
Dependency – The wealthy rely on their family wealth.
Insatiable Curiosity – This is an age of exploration
Obligation – Rich or poor, everyone has a part to play and a responsibility to keep.

DEVICES AND GADGETS

The Victorian era is an age of science and invention. Every day, new marvels appear, some even appearing alien to the uninitiated. Scientific shows demonstrate electrical power, steam-driven machinery and all manner of new understanding. There is plenty for a Boffin to do, whether it's building their own strange devices in the pursuit of science, or trying to make sense of actual alien technology and wondrous gadgets from the future.

The rules for creating a new Gadget remain unchanged in the Victorian age (see the **Doctor Who Roleplaying Game Core Rulebook**). In some cases this might be an advanced device built with Victorian technology. In others this might be an innovation so strange even its creator does not truly understand what it does. Of course, in such an environment, the odd piece of truly advanced or alien technology might go unnoticed amidst the fugue of oddments and eccentric appliances.

STYLE OF DEVICES

Victorian Gadgets are often built of wood and brass. Metalworking is expensive and so is usually either done on a tiny or industrial scale, making it unsuitable for most personal gadgets (the Bulky trait is particularly suitable for such gadgets). However, a skilled woodworker can create boxes and containers that are both functional and pleasing to the eye, for a comparatively low cost compared to metalworker. Metal brackets or brass ornamentation can then be fitted to add strength and a little extra flair.

Remember that invention is not something the poor can usually afford. This is especially true for amateur artificers, who require custom-built containers and parts. While it is easy to find highly skilled craftsmen, their services do not come cheaply. Most devices tend to look stylish as well as perform their function. If it would not look well placed at a dinner party, the invention is not really finished.

TYPES OF TECHNOLOGY

When considering the look and style of your device, you should also give some thought as to what is powering it. While nuclear power remains a long way off and the internal combustion is in its infancy, there are plenty of different styles of invention that you might specialise in. Each has their own advantages and disadvantages, and more importantly their own particular style when used to create inventions.

Clockwork is a tried and tested mechanism (and will make a resurgence in the 51st century). The development of the pocket watch has allowed the creation of some incredibly intricate devices using a series of cogs and springs. Clockwork has the advantage in that it requires no exterior power source and that it can power small and precise devices. However, it must be wound up often, and cannot create a lot of motive power.

Steam power has become synonymous with the age. Steam trains thunder across the country and steam engines drive the heart of industry. Steam is relatively cheap, essentially requiring a boiler to burn coal and create pressurised steam. This steam, when forced into pistons can drive machinery. A single steam power source might even drive several machines at the same time. The problem with steam power is that it is big and heavy, and requires constant fuel. It does deliver a great deal of motive force though making it very efficient, if a little noisy and messy.

Electricity is the new wonder of the age. Arguments rage over alternate or direct current as the best use of this frightening and magical power. Electrical displays are dramatic, and appear as if the power of the storm has been harnessed. Unfortunately, electrical power can only be delivered in the form of batteries, which are quite large and heavy. However, even an advanced electrical device might be charged from Victorian electrical power.

Gas is a common fixture in Victorian London, providing heat and light across the city. As a power source it is only an ignition system. But advanced technology might use its vapourous qualities as a form of transmission. Gas is readily available, but also highly flammable, making devices powered by it somewhat unstable.

Victorian scientists posited the idea that the 'ether' was an invisible and intangible medium that allowed light to travel – rather than being disproved as a theory, perhaps alien creatures might make use of it. As a source of power, the ether might allow light to be bent, twisted or focused, possibly even into an energy weapon. Ether-powered devices might require all manner of odd buttons, dials and antenna to capture this insubstantial energy and turn them into something useful. Etheric devices will be among the most strange and distinct of all new technology.

TECHNOLOGY LEVEL

The Tech Level of the Victorian era (and therefore of adventurers native to the 19th century) is 4. However, some alien characters might have a higher Tech Level if they come from a more advanced society (or the future)

THE DOCTOR'S VICTORIAN COMPANIONS

As we've already explored, the Doctor has had many adventures in Victorian times, and whenever he's done so it's been in the company of companions from that era. This next section describes some of the Doctor's Victorian companions, as well as providing advice as to how you might use them as the basis for their own particular campaign. You might simply want to use them as a quick way to dive straight into adventure, or you might want to play in a campaign with the same sort of feel, but with new characters of your own.

THE PATERNOSTER GANG

The Doctor has always been adept at finding the lost and the lonely and giving them purpose. The Paternoster Gang are no exception, and each recognises the debt they owe. The group began with Madame Vastra, a Silurian. She was woken from hibernation by construction work on the London underground. She awoke angry and confused and killed several people before the Doctor found her. Once calm and focused, Vastra felt she needed to make amends for what she had done, and the Doctor helped her settle into a new life as a London noblewoman. As part of her new life she employed a housemaid called Jenny Flint. Their relationship grew deeper than just mistress and employee and they became lovers and eventually married. Jenny quickly took to a new life of investigation and crime fighting, and proved an adept student of Vastra's weapon skills. After the battle of Demon's Run the pair added a third member to the group in the shape of the disgraced Sontarren called Strax. Strax simply had nowhere to go, but loved the idea of adventure and battle, although he still takes his job as a nurse very seriously.

The Paternoster Gang have fought several terrible enemies together. As such they have become renowned as the people to come to when the authorities cannot help. While many people think them odd, no one truly believes that half the group are not even human. So the gang has a good reputation with several levels of society, and offer their help to rich and poor. Their status is such that when they appear on the scene, even the police defer to their judgement.

While the gang have fought several enemies of their own, they have always stood ready to assist the Doctor. They all came to his aid at Demon's Run, in payment of old debts. When the Doctor retired to London to mourn the loss of Amy and Rory, they did their best to shake him out of his depression. Later the Doctor came to their aid as they investigated the Crimson Horror. After this they began an investigation into the rumours of Trenzalore, leading the Doctor to face both the end of his timeline and the Great Intelligence once more.

Most recently they helped the Doctor (and Clara) deal with his new regeneration when the TARDIS brought him and a dinosaur back to London. So it is often the case that the Doctor joins their investigations rather than them assisting him in his. They are his valued friends, and loyal agents, and together they are more than equal to any problem.

Character sheets for Madame Vastra, Jenny Flint and Strax can be found on pgs. 117-119.

Paternoster Investigations

The Paternoster Gang are drawn to the strange and unusual, and have a reputation for being able to solve cases thought unsolvable. The cases they take on often begin with the oddest mystery, which turns out to be even stranger upon investigation.

Paternoster investigations are not always adventures of heroics and bravado. They are investigators first, following the clues just like Sherlock Holmes (whose methods are likely based on theirs) might do. What appears impossible, might turn out to be eminently probable once a keen mind and careful observation is employed – and the existence of aliens taken into account.

The Paternoster Campaign, beginning on pg. 91, takes a much more in-depth look at running adventures in the style of the Paternoster Gang.

THE FURTHER ADVENTURES OF JACKSON LAKE

The Doctor can't be everywhere, and sometimes someone else needs to step forward to face the darkness. Jackson Lake took up this responsibility quite by accident when he encountered the Cybermen in his home. After seeing his wife killed and his son, Frederick, kidnapped, Jackson was exposed to a Cyberman Infostamp containing information about the Doctor. His mind coped with the trauma by assuming the identity of the Doctor. He even gained a companion in Rosita Farisi, after rescuing her from another Cyberman attack.

Jackson Lake's adventures with the Doctor take place in 1851, but **Paternoster Investigations** is set at least 40 years later. The Gamemaster might like to blur the lines of history and have him accompany the Paternoster Gang on their adventures, or to set the campaign earlier on in the Victorian age. But even many years later Jackson's legacy may remain. Even as an old man he might still remain a valued advisor to the Paternoster Gang; he may have even been instrumental in helping establish the Pasternoster Gang as his successors. His son Frederick, now middle aged himself, may have taken up his father's mantle. Perhaps he stalks the streets as another lone agent against the shadows?

Character sheets for Jackson Lake and Rosita Farisi can be found on pgs. 120-121.

The Jackson Lake Campaign

Adventures in the style of Jackson Lake are about a heroic inventor taking on the unknown, accompanied by intrepid companions. Jackson is a gentleman who has gathered the help he needs to defend England from injustice. He is not a careful investigator, but a daring hero who would rather throw a lasso around a Cybershade than secretly follow it to its lair. Why, it sounds just like an adventure the Doctor might embark upon!

Such a campaign would also perfectly suit an actual Time Lord, but one marooned on Earth in the Victorian age. Perhaps he has been exiled here, or is trying to repair his TARDIS so he can leave. He might also have decided to stay and right a particular wrong, possibly one he was responsible for when he first arrived. Such adventures might include similar conflicts to those the Third Doctor dealt with in his time trapped on Earth.

JAGO AND LITEFOOT INVESTIGATE

Sometimes, even when they are hopelessly underskilled or underprepared, certain people can't quite let go of a life of adventure after meeting the Doctor. Professor Litefoot and theatrical impresario Henry Gordon Jago are two such unlikely heroes.

After helping the Doctor face down Magnus Greel (see ***The Talons of Weng Chiang*** in **The Fourth Doctor Sourcebook**) they have formed an unlikely duo so they might root out wrongdoing in the heart of London.

Jago and Litefoot are the epitome of the middle class adventurer. Both are wealthy gentlemen, but neither has ties to the nobility. They are both in over their heads when it comes to hunting down the bad guys, but armed with good old fashioned British pluck, they somehow manage to muddle through. They might get in the way of the likes of the Paternoster Gang as much as they might offer help, but they don't give up on a case just because things get a little difficult.

Character sheets for Jago and Litefoot can be found on pgs. 122-123.

The Jago and Litefoot Campaign

These investigative adventurers are for characters with little or no special abilities or powers, and might be played for laughs as much as adventure as there is a lot of potential comedy. Quite often these amateur heroes will find they have bitten off far more than they can chew.

But as gentlemen they refuse to walk away when there is justice to be done. The group will also have less experience with the more alien cases, and will be left bamboozled by creatures from other worlds. But even if the beast has tentacles and powerful technology, Jago and Litefoot know a villain when they see one!

THE MANY FACES OF CLARA OSWALD

There are countless splinters of Clara Oswald scattered across time. So it should come as no surprise that one (or more than one – see also pg. 72) appeared in the 19th century. Fashioning herself a new identity as Miss Montegue, she became a governess for the Latimer family. Captain Latimer had recently lost his wife and the children, Francesca and Digby, took to Clara instantly.

An encounter with the Doctor and the Great Intelligence led to Clara losing her life. But what if she had not? We could imagine that a woman with such an inquiring mind might become a great ally of the Paternoster Gang. With contacts across two levels of society she would be a great asset, and might quickly have become the fourth member of the group.

A character sheet for Clara Oswin Oswald can be found on pg. 124.

The Victorian Clara Campaign

As a companion, Clara is the perfect model for a Victorian character – she is smart, adventurous and inquisitive, and defies expectations set before her as a working class Victorian girl by living a secret life as a governess to a wealthy family.

While her adventuring career was cut short saving the Doctor from the Ice Governess, we might like to imagine a campaign in which she was saved by Strax. Presumably she would have gone adventuring with the Doctor, but she might also have remained in London, perhaps gaining her own set of companions and having her own adventures, much like the real Clara ended up doing. A campaign in this fashion might look a lot like one featuring the Paternosters.

A VICTORIAN OUT OF TIME

Not every Victorian adventurer needs to stay in the Victorian era – one great example of such a character is Victoria Waterfield. Victoria became the Doctor's companion when she was involved in a Dalek plot as a hostage.

Vicroria was held prisoner to ensure her father, Professor Edward Waterfield, continued to work for them (see ***The Evil of the Daleks*** in **The Second Doctor Sourcebook**). The Daleks were defeated, but Victoria had lost her family, her home; everything in fact. She had little left to lose but to join the Doctor on his adventures. Her new life was something of a departure for her. She faced Cybermen, Yetis, Ice Warriors and evil duplicates of the Doctor and finally saved the world by screaming at seaweed. Most of the places she visited were also very cold and covered in ice. So she never quite got to see the universe at its best.

While a life spent travelling time and space might seem odd for a well brought-up Victorian woman, Victoria takes to it well after a fashion. She is the epitome of her age in this regard. At first she is shocked and confused by the different views and morals of each new place (and the attire of some of the ladies), but she is also fascinated by new cultures and eager to see what lies around the next corner. For Victoria, her adventures are a 'grand tour', but one that takes her to places unimagined.

Eventually, she decides to leave the Doctor. Like many Victorians, it is a home life and family that she really craves. While adventure is all very well, there must come a time to return home and settle down.

A character sheet for Victoria Waterfield can be found on pg. 125.

The Victoria Waterfield Campaign

If you are playing a Victorian character travelling with a Time Lord, Victoria will be your first stop for inspiration. While there may be a lot of screaming, Victoria is more than just a damsel in distress. She is as brave and stalwart as the Doctor's other companions, and gradually learns to overcome her fears and confusion. She could have remained hidden in the TARDIS until she found a safe place, but her natural curiosity brings her out to face her fears.

But what if Victoria had taken after her father a little more? Might she have become a scientist herself? A little shocking perhaps, but not unknown in the era. Her father created a functional time machine with his friend Theodore Maxwell, bringing them to the attention of the Daleks. But what if the Daleks hadn't interrupted them, or if Victoria had continued their work – what Victorian adventurer needs a Time Lord if they have a time machine of their own?

Victoria, her father and Maxwell (or another group of Victorian characters) might set off to explore time and space by themselves. Without the advice of an experienced time traveller (like the Doctor) what scrapes might they get themselves into? Would they simply seek to study new cultures, or begin to colonise far-flung worlds? As they encounter more advanced species, they might learn to create more advanced temporal devices. If they share this technology, might the British Empire stretch out across the universe in great steam-powered temporal devices?

THE PATERNOSTER CAMPAIGN

THE PATERNOSTER CAMPAIGN

The Doctor Who Roleplaying Game does a fantastic job of teaching you the basics of playing a roleplaying game as well as designing adventures of the sort that a certain Time Lord might find familiar. But, while the Doctor's adventures take place in all of time and space, Paternoster adventures are generally confined to one era – that of London in 189X. It is Great Britain at the height of the empire, when the sun never sets on it and it is widely considered the greatest power in the world.

This chapter is designed to help you craft adventures that the Paternoster Gang might find themselves joining, with or without the Doctor's help. Let's look at a few ways in which a typical Paternoster adventure might be distinguished from one more typical of the Doctor and the TARDIS.

IT'S A TEAM EFFORT

In contrast to the model of a super-competent Time Lord and their companions that many games of the **Doctor Who Roleplaying Game** follow, Paternoster adventures assume that the players' characters are all relatively equal members of a team. While it is certainly possible to follow the former model, with one player playing the super-competent 'consulting detective' and the other players essentially their companions, the presumption here is that each member of your own Paternoster Gang brings something to the table that the others lack (as well as weaknesses for which the other Paternosters need to compensate!).

Players should bear this in mind when designing their own characters; no one Paternoster should be capable of doing everything, and characters who specialise in a particular niche will be more effective for it since they aren't spreading their points too thin. Similarly, you should be taking into account the particular strengths and weaknesses of each Paternoster when creating your adventures so that each can meaningfully contribute to its success (or bear the responsibility for its failure!).

HOW CAPABLE?

Of course, the first question that arises when talking about strengths and weaknesses is how capable should an individual Paternoster be? Is it OK to be a great detective, a medical doctor, and a good fighter? Is it OK to be a technical expert and a social butterfly? The answer, of course, depends on how big your Paternoster Gang is.

When designing Paternoster characters, you'll want to separate the things everyone should be able to do from the things that you only want one Paternoster to be able to do. If, for example, you plan to make investigation and action key elements in your adventures, then every Paternoster should be able to handle at least basic investigations and hold their own when engaged in fisticuffs. Conversely, you may only see medicine, science, technology and social interaction as fields only a particular Paternoster should be proficient with. Of course, if you only have three players, then you'll want each Paternoster to specialise in two fields, or else leave those fields to be handled by the Paternoster Irregulars (see pg. 46).

Let's use the classic Paternoster Gang of Madame Vastra, Jenny Flint and Strax as an example. They often tend to get involved in action scenes, so all three are capable at fighting. Individually, Madame Vastra is the cunning detective, Jenny is the servant who easily blends in and Strax is a medical nurse and driver. The use of these abilities are peppered throughout an adventure, giving each of them a chance to shine in ways the others can't.

TEMPORALLY TETHERED

Perhaps the most exciting thing about the Doctor's adventures is that they can take place anywhere in time and space. One adventure he's crossing the Rubicon with Julius Caesar, the next he's preventing the Sontarans from interfering with World War IV, and the one after that he's across the universe helping a space colony defend themselves from the Daleks in the far future . No two adventures need look alike and each time, save for the occasional return somewhere they've already visited, the Doctor and his companions have to introduce themselves each time they step out of the TARDIS into a new world.

By contrast, Paternoster adventures take place in immediate chronological order at a single point in space. At first blush, this may seem quite limiting, as the Paternosters always find themselves in and around London in the waning years of the Victorian era. However, what this does is allow for rich and powerful storytelling, as the Paternosters have time to cultivate relationships and flesh out their corner of time and space. Perhaps more importantly, they must deal with the consequences of their actions.

This last point is very important. The Doctor can overthrow an alien dictator and foment a popular revolution, but there is nothing keeping him from popping back into the TARDIS and leaving the fallout to those left in his wake. The Paternosters don't have that luxury. If they fail to foil an assassination attempt or cause part of London to go up in flames, then they may be called to account or at least have their reputations suffer for it. If they've done something that could conceivably alter the timeline then they'll be tasked with fixing it (unless you determine that they're in a parallel timeline, of course...).

For the most part, keeping the same setting from adventure to adventure means that you can integrate

THE OCCASIONAL FLIGHT OF FANCY

Just because you're running a **Paternoster Investigations** campaign doesn't mean that your players won't occasionally see the wider universe of time and space, especially if you have a great idea for an adventure that just doesn't mesh well with the Victorian setting. You never know when the Doctor or a Time Agent may have need of their services, or perhaps your characters uncover (or invent!) a mysterious time machine in the course of their adventures that transports them somewhere else, and they have to undertake a local adventure before they get back. In fact, time travel need not be involved at all; exploring Silurian caves or flying to the Moon to stop an invasion make for a great change of pace entirely in keeping with the genre!

If you'd like a longer diversion between Victorian adventures you can even make trying to get home part of a mini-campaign. This can be a lot of fun so long as you don't run afoul of the 'bait-and-switch'; if your players relish the idea of playing Victorian adventurers they may not appreciate your switch to a more 'traditional' campaign, especially when it seems like Victorian London is getting further and further away!

your Paternoster Gang into a living, breathing world. Today's victim could be tomorrow's Irregular; today's ally could be tomorrow's rival. A Paternoster who belongs to a gentlemen's club may find their list of contacts growing over time, while a Paternoster who crosses a powerful underworld figure may find obstacles placed in their way on future adventures...

A VICTORIAN CONCEIT

As discussed on pg. 8, **Paternoster Investigations** takes place in the last decade of the 19th century, but that's not really all that important. You probably already have a general idea of what London life looked like in the late Victorian era and that will be enough to paint a picture for your players. It doesn't really matter whether a character dons a bowler or stovepipe hat or which Prime Minister is currently residing in 10 Downing Street (more on that in a moment!). Don't let yourself get bogged down in minutiae and concentrate on creating a fun story!

What *is* important is that these adventures primarily take place in Victorian London and evoke a general sense of the Victorian age at a time when Britain was ostensibly the master of the world. The sun never set on the British Empire and yet in spite of that there was still much social, economic and political inequality. From our future lens, it doesn't matter much whether bowler hats or bustles were in fashion in the 1890s; if it feels right then we simply roll with it.

A similar approach is taken with real historical figures. In **Paternoster Investigations** we take the approach that the inclusion of real historical figures are actually fictionalised analogues whom you can adapt to fit the needs of a particular adventure. Sometimes this means adjusting their age or 'massaging' the dates when they made notable contributions to history to better fit in with your adventure. This does have its limits; while it's unlikely you'd get away with having Charles Dickens walking around London in the 1890s (as he'd been dead for 20 years or more by then!), you could easily contrive to involve HG Wells or Arthur Conan Doyle!

In order to drive this point home, we've taken a page from some of the Doctor's 'modern' adventures and created a fictional British Prime Minister. Nathan Fairfield, 8th Earl of Redbury, is a composite of the various real Prime Ministers who served in the last decade of the 19th century and his inclusion is a signal to the players that history is not necessarily set in stone; anything can happen as a result of their actions or their failures.

GREATER LATITUDE WITH CONCEITS

Ordinarily, a Silurian walking into a 1950s American diner or a Sontaran strolling into King Louis XIV's court is going to cause heads to turn and accusations of aliens or demons walking amongst us to fly! In **Paternoster Investigations**, however, Madame Vastra is able to hand-wave her alien-ness by claiming that she has a bad skin condition and no one thinks twice about Strax's potato-shaped head. Similarly, the residents of London seem to take giant Cybermen and dinosaurs stomping through the city in their stride. Even Scotland Yard seems used to dealing with some very alien situations.

A large part of the fun in playing Paternoster adventures is the ability to take an alien, make them a player character, and set them loose in Victorian London as if they were going to a fancy dress party, and the hilarious situations that result from the alien not quite understanding late Victorian society. This can be diminished if every time an alien character shows their face they're driven out of London by mobs wielding torches and pitchforks.

Presuming that a Paternoster character could pass for a human in bad light (Strax, for example) then it's probably OK to let them walk around the city without a disguise and only token references to their strange appearance.

Paternosters who are humanoid but obviously not human (like Madame Vastra) should be encouraged to make minimal effort to disguise themselves enough for other characters to wink away their alien-ness; Vastra, for example, claims a skin condition and wears a veil when in public. Only aliens that are obviously non-humanoid would need some type of holographic disguise to hide their true appearance.

Similarly, Paternoster adventures rarely impose the full weight of social prejudices that were prevalent in the actual historical era. No one bats an eye at a woman being a private investigator, for example, let alone when that same female investigator claims that she is married to a woman.

This conceit frees the players up to create whatever types of characters they want. While it's certainly OK to touch upon these societal norms as a plot point in a given adventure, the players should never feel punished for playing a particular character.

CREATING PATERNOSTER ADVENTURES

So how does one go about creating a Paternoster adventure? Is it simply aliens in deerstalker hats solving mysteries or is there more to it than that? This section takes a look at what makes a good 'Paternoster adventure' and what distinguishes it from standard Victorian fare. It's designed to get you into the mindset of getting inspiration for your adventures to best ensure that they fit the Paternoster mould. What you won't get here is a detailed analysis of what makes a good adventure because that is exhaustively covered in both the **Doctor Who Roleplaying Game Core Rulebook** and the **Gamemaster's Companion.** While a Paternoster adventure has its own distinctive feel, it is still first and foremost an adventure that the Doctor and his companions would be comfortable tackling.

REVERSING THE POLARITY OF THE NEUTRON FLOW

The Occasional Flight of Fancy discussed taking your Paternoster Gang out of Victorian London and into other times and places. The reverse is also possible: you can bring your time and space travelling player characters to late Victorian London for an exciting adventure!

Much of the material in this supplement can be used as a quasi-historical sourcebook to provide interesting characters and plot hooks for your time-travelling characters to interact with. They might still run afoul of the Torchwood Institute, uncover the machinations of the Napoleon of Crime, or help Prime Minister Fairfield foil an alien invasion. You could even bring in a Paternoster or two as 'guest stars' – perhaps Strax is on hand to help them out of a difficult situation or Jackson Lake remembers a key bit of information that is useful to them!

ALIENS IN LONDON

One common thread that defines Paternoster adventures is that the Paternoster Gang is usually employed against other aliens. Clockwork Robots, dinosaurs, the Great Intelligence, and the Red Leech were all creatures that, if not technically 'alien' in some cases, certainly didn't belong in the 19th century! It's the introduction of the alien that sets Paternoster adventures apart from the standard mysteries of the late Victorian period; after all, it doesn't take a Silurian and a Sontaran to sniff out the truth behind the Red-Headed League or figure out why someone is painting dogs with luminescent paint?

Whether your particular Paternoster Gang is well-suited for investigations or not, they are probably the best equipped at dealing with alien threats, which are usually out of the league of local authorities. The Paternosters have access to advanced knowledge and technologies and can more easily recognise alien threats for what they are.

Thus, when designing a Paternoster adventure, the first thing you should do is decide what alien threat drives the plot. This may be an actual alien, such as the Cybermen or Missy, or it may be something home-grown but out of the ordinary, like a scientific genius creating a technological marvel or a hypnotist using her psychic powers to overthrow the government. It could also be a piece of alien technology that has been unearthed and is now being used towards sinister ends.

Don't let the Victorian setting fool you; any of these threats would operate in exactly the same way whether it be 1896, 1966 or 2016. Cybermen might be trying to convert the population, the Sycorax will be trying to conquer the planet and Missy may be stirring up trouble in the hopes of getting a rise out of her 'boyfriend.' Just as UNIT called on the Doctor the moment something strange was discovered, so too will Scotland Yard call the Paternoster Gang!

LITERARY INSPIRATION

We've name-checked Sherlock Holmes several times in this chapter (and previously – see pg. 20) and that's no accident; the Great Detective has become ubiquitous throughout this period of British history and it can be difficult at times to think of creating Victorian adventures that are anything but a consulting detective mystery with an alien spin. In fact, there are numerous other authors from whom to draw inspiration other than Sir Arthur Conan Doyle.

HG Wells is an obvious source. *The Invisible Man, The Island of Doctor Moreau* and *The Time Machine* all posit technological breakthroughs that could inspire plots with which to menace the Paternosters (Mary Shelley's *Frankenstein, or the Modern Prometheus* also fits this mould) and *The War of the Worlds* posits an alien invasion that quickly gets out of hand. See also pgs. 13 and 28 for more about HG Wells.

Robert Louis Stevenson's *Strange Case of Dr Jekyll and Mr Hyde* is also a great source of inspiration for shape-shifting threats. Bram Stoker's *Dracula* is the quintessential vampire story and is essentially an adventure about trying to contain an alien 'virus' before it spreads. W Grove's *A Mexican Mystery* and its sequel, *The Wreck of a World*, is one of the earliest 'machine revolution' stories, with self-aware locomotives attacking humanity.

A STEAMPUNK LENS

While it's not strictly necessary to maintain a 'steampunk' aesthetic, it's evocative of the genre to have your aliens using technology largely built from wood, brass and iron, belching steam from boilers, and floating amongst the clouds rather than racing through them. This is especially true of aliens who find themselves trapped on Earth and have to adapt the local technology to suit their purposes.

Evoking the steampunk aesthetic also involves highlighting social inequities, with the working classes covered in soot and grease as they toil to build and maintain steam engines that the well-dressed upper classes get to enjoy. The industrial revolution is an age of marvels, but it is also pushing the masses towards revolution. Aliens smart enough to tap into that discontent can gain powerful and unwitting allies for their own nefarious plans.

A word of caution, while the 'steampunk era' is often equated with the Victorian, Paternoster adventures take place in the 1890s. While it can be tempting to exclusively showcase boffins and aliens relying on steam engines to power their machines, it's important to note that other technologies, including electricity and oil, are on the rise. Indeed, throughout the 1890s one is as likely to encounter a 'horseless carriage' powered by an electric battery or petrol as a steam engine.

THE ART OF DEDUCTION, OR LACK THEREOF

It is deceptively easy to treat Paternoster adventures as Sherlock Holmesian cases, but with Silurians and Sontarans in place of great detectives. In fact, there is nothing wrong with this approach if that is how you want to run the game! Putting that aside, however, there are several things to consider before you hand out deerstalker caps and Meerschaum pipes to all your players.

Firstly, this is the **Doctor Who Roleplaying Game**, not **Late Victorian Mysteries**. It's more likely that your players are interested in playing fish-out-of-water characters in a Victorian setting, not necessarily digging for clues and interviewing witnesses in the hopes of discovering the key piece of evidence to advance the plot forward – Strax is more likely to stomp all over such situations! They'll certainly expect some investigation – the pull of the genre is strong – but they may still be looking for a conventional time-and-space romp in Victoriana.

Secondly, even if your players are looking forward to Victorian mystery-solving, they probably won't be doing it as standard locals; they'll be doing it as aliens with advanced knowledge, sonic screwdrivers, bio-medical scanners and universal smart phones. In other words, they'll have a lot more tools at their disposal than a typical late Victorian detective. These gadgets must be considered if you don't want your mystery to fall apart in the first three seconds because the murderer is really a camouflaged alien and you forgot to take into account that the sonic screwdriver could deactivate the camouflage!

Given these two points, you'll have to decide as the Gamemaster whether your Paternoster adventures are going to focus on Victorian mysteries or typical Doctor Who-ish derring-do. There is a happy medium between the two where the Paternosters fit perfectly, and that's as a deconstruction of Holmesian style mysteries.

What makes the Paternosters work so well as detectives is their access to advanced knowledge and technology which enables them to solve crimes in ways no Victorian could fathom! In an amusing nod to great detectives of the past the Paternosters may even rely on 'rational deductions' to cover up – or at least relieve the need to explain – their advanced methodology.

Still, how you allow your players to utilise advanced technology is going to have a great impact on how mysteries are conducted or even if they are feasible. If, for example, a Paternoster can use a hair follicle to scan for a kidnap victim's location in the city, then the investigation is going to take a very different course than if the Paternosters actually had to discover his location! In a 'pure' investigative campaign you might want to limit scans and other abilities from trumping mystery plot points, while in campaigns that don't revolve around mysteries you might be more apt to let gadgets short-cut investigations.

There is a middle path, however. London is a large city with roughly 4.5 million inhabitants – it could take time – perhaps hours or days - for a scanner set on a particular genetic signature to find a single person and even then it may only be able to nail down a particular neighbourhood, building, or room. Aliens and advanced humans might be good at camouflaging themselves, fooling scanners and even putting out false signatures. Finally, particularly crafty aliens may even use a technological dampener; something that stops electronics from working would go undetected by the local authorities in Victorian London!

It's also possible for you to ease your players into a more investigative campaign by having them experience the thrill of aliens short-circuiting traditional Victorian mysteries easily at first, only to find later investigations made more difficult by villains growing accustomed to their methods and using various means to counter them. In addition, the Paternosters come to rely on 'Irregulars' with talents not normally needed by Scotland Yard in order to discover new methods of subterfuge.

NEW USES FOR OLD SKILLS

No matter how 'investigative' your adventures turn out to be, there are going to be times when your players are going to want to roll for something and none of the skills seem quite right. When this happens, don't worry! Simply decide what the character is trying to do and make an appropriate attribute and skill pairing that fits.

A STUDY IN FLAX

A STUDY IN FLAX

A STUDY IN FLAX

In this adventure a time traveller from Earth's future, Professor Fiora Breen, finds herself stranded in the past, the ordeal rendering her genetic code unstable. Horrified and realising that she will never survive a trip back to the future, Breen is attempting to fix the problem before risking a trip back home. Unfortunately, this requires her to steal life energy from her victims.

Napoleon is a partner in crime in this venture, as he sees an opportunity to create a new Time Corridor. While Earth lacks the resources to build such a gadget, Napoleon believes that Professor Breen's Time Cabinet can be modified to approximate one, presuming that she can eliminate the problem inherent in using it. To this end, Napoleon's minions are helping Professor Breen procure the resources that she needs, including fresh victims. The experiment has also caught the eye of Dr Karfelov, who has his own designs on a time machine...

ADVENTURE SYNOPSIS

The characters are employed to help find Ellen Terry, an actress who disappeared shortly after the final curtain closed during a performance of *King Arthur*. While Lyceum owner and lead actor Henry Irving believes a rival playwright, George Bernard Shaw, to be responsible, the truth is more sinister. Ms Terry seems to share certain physical characteristics with several other disappearances over the last few months, most of whom were fished out of the Thames. During the course of the investigation, however, Ms Terry is discovered safe and sound near Shaw's residence. The characters' investigations take them all over London, from the Shaw residence in St James to a poor house in Bermondsey, and even to Leper Hall. Over the course of their investigation the characters discover the true purpose behind the abductions and killings: a time traveller from the future is trying to repair her genetic code!

The finale takes place in a warehouse on the Isle of Dogs, where 51st century time traveller Professor Breen is busy perfecting her time machine, while using a gadget provided by the mysterious Dr Karfelov (see pg. 75) to stabilise her genetic code. Not only do the characters have to deal with the desperate time traveller (and possibly Dr Karfelov), but also the Napoleon of Crime, as the crafty Dalek needs both of these engineers to further his own criminal schemes...

THE ZYGMA EXPERIMENTS

Mankind finally developed time travel in the 51st century but the path to get there was not easy. The earliest attempts, aided by the Supreme Alliance of Eastern States' Minister of Justice Magnus Greel, relied on the use of Zygma Beams to power Time

Cabinets. Unfortunately, use of such Zygma Beams mutated the time traveller and could eventually cause a devastating implosion. Professor Fiora Breen, one of the earliest engineers attached to the project, believed that she had accounted for the radiation and volunteered to take a Time Cabinet back through time to test her equipment. She couldn't have been more wrong. Not only did she burn out her Time Cabinet, but she also suffered the effects of genetic breakdown. Fortunately for her the disturbance of Artron energy attracted Napoleon's attention, and the criminal Dalek offered to help in return for her services. With little choice, Breen accepted the deal and Napoleon contacted Dr Karfelov to help stabilise her in return for her building a functioning time machine for Napoleon.

Dr Karfelov's treatment relied on notes stolen from New Scotland Yard's archives regarding the 'Chinese Doll Murders' case several years earlier. In order to keep her appearance as normal as possible,she needs to use victims that have similar genetic markers; specifically flaxen-haired, grey-eyed women like Professor Breen herself. Unfortunatley, the process is fatal to the donor.

Understanding the horror of what she is doing, Breen rationalises it to herself by only choosing victims who have no futures; she is doing this only in the name of science and of saving her future from the horrors of faulty time travel, as Breen theorises that the damage caused by Zygma Beams occurs on both ends. Prolonged use from the 51st century would eventually tear the Earth apart!

Fortunately – and unbeknownst to Breen – the Doctor does offer temporal assistance in her timeline. At the conclusion of World War VI, the Doctor warned against using Zygma Beams and dropped a few hints on how to create effective time travel. While advancement happened slower than some would like it does eventually succeed and lead to the creation of the Time Agency.

1. QUEEN GUINEVERE IS MISSING!

This adventure begins early in the morning, possibly even before breakfast. Someone arrives at one of the character's doors with an urgent case – the female lead of a play – *King Arthur* – has gone missing! If the characters have the Friends (Police), Agent of Scotland Yard or similar traits, then Inspector Gregson (see pg. 50) or another of their police contacts engages their services directly; if not then it is possible that Bram Stoker or one of the play's other investors contacts them. If she is an NPC known to the group (rather than a character herself), Madame Vastra may ask them to look into this affair on her behalf as something more pressing has come up for her that involves a strange blue box...

In any event, their 'employer' gives them the basic facts of the case. Ellen Terry, who portrays Guinevere in King Arthur at the Lyceum (given its prestige and the fact that the music was written by Sullivan it's possible that one or more of the characters have seen a previous performance) has gone missing. Foul play is suspected, but there are no leads beyond Ms Terry

simply deciding to disappear after seeing a not-so-secret admirer (if pressed, the employer tells them that an Irish playwright may be involved). Given a few odd occurrences that evening, the characters have been called upon to see if they could shed any light on the situation.

CLUES AT THE LYCEUM

Obviously, the first place that the characters are going to want to visit is the Lyceum, which is owned by its leading actor, Henry Irving. As might be expected, there is a lot of excitement and worry as those involved with the play are worried about what happened to Ms Terry, while at the same time scrambling to get her understudy, her own daughter Edith Craig, up to speed.

The characters are met at the door by manager Bram Stoker who thanks them for coming so quickly and hopes they can assist. He claims that he has no idea what could have happened to her but a character making an Awareness + Convince roll (Difficulty 12) can sense that he's holding something back. What he's holding back is something of an open secret: Irving, his employer, and Ms Terry are lovers and Terry received a bouquet last night that likely came from a rival. He also mentions that some staff saw Terry leave the building via the alley. Once the characters enter the theatre, Irving looks both annoyed and delighted to see them. He knows who is behind this and the first statement out of his mouth is "Finally, you're here! I trust then that the police have Mr Shaw in custody and that muck snipe has confessed?'

THEATRE IS POLITICS

While everyone is worried about Ellen Terry's disappearance, they assume she spent the night with her lover, whom most presume is George Bernard Shaw. It's widely known that Irving and Terry had more than a professional relationship, although Irving's attentions have waned over the last couple of years (something Terry attributed to her advanced age; she is approaching 50), so it's little wonder that another admirer might steal her away.

George Bernard Shaw is an Irish theatre critic and playwright who recently began corresponding with Terry. She enjoys the attention, although Irving believes that Shaw has a professional objective; Shaw writes modern plays and he has been openly critical of the Shakespearean performances at the Lyceum. Irving believes that Shaw wants Terry for himself, both as a leading actress for his plays and as a consort. Unfortunately, Shaw was not in attendance last night and Terry absconded with the note that came with the flowers. Stoker went to Shaw's residence late last night to collect Terry and was told that she was not there.

INTERVIEWING HENRY IRVING

As both the theatre's owner and its leading actor, the characters will likely interview Henry Irving. Irving is genuinely concerned about Terry, but doesn't mention that they are romantically involved; he is too much of a professional (any time travelling character who makes an Ingenuity + Knowledge roll at Difficulty 15 will recall that he is due to be knighted within a

few months; the first actor to receive the honour) and still married.

Characters who succeed at an Awareness + Convince roll (Difficulty 12) can tell that Irving is obviously perturbed. Irving has an intense ego and the thought of someone else 'stealing' Terry away from him is eating him up. It also shows in his line recitals with Edith; he is being quite flirty, almost as if to convince himself that he is still charismatic.

Irving tells the characters that he hasn't seen Terry since the final curtain call yesterday evening. He felt something was amiss when he saw a bouquet of flowers on a table that contained an envelope – the card was missing – with her name on it. He suspected Shaw and sent a stagehand, Malcolm Wade, to warn Shaw that his poaching would not be tolerated. Needless to say, Irving grew quite cross when Terry didn't join him for a post-performance dinner as she'd promised.

Irving later sent Bram Stoker to the Shaw residence to "remind her of her previous engagement" but Stoker was turned away at the door by Shaw's mother, who claimed that her son had retired early, alone. She confirms he's been in his room all day (this is true; Shaw is suffering from a bad cold).

Wade didn't return for several minutes, but when he did he looked quite dirty and dishevelled. The young man claimed that he was looking for her in the alley and he stumbled. He claimed that she was nowhere to be found. If asked where Mr Wade is now, Irving gets irritated and notes that the stagehand is still lucky to be employed as Irving suspects he was probably distracted by the 'Exeter angels'; prostitutes that prey on both theatre and lecture hall patrons. In any case, Wade is probably at his home, since the stage crew isn't due to arrive until after luncheon.

BURLEIGH STREET

The Lyceum sits on the corner of the Strand and Wellington Street, facing the latter. Exeter Street runs across the side opposite the Strand and wraps around Exeter Hall, a grand lecture hall owned by Lord Shaftesbury. Between the two buildings sits Burleigh Street, and it is here that Ms Terry was last seen.

Characters looking for clues in Burleigh Street may, with an Awareness + Science roll (Difficulty 12) notice a pool of Morphic residue in the middle of the street. If the character is familiar with aliens, then they may make an Ingenuity + Science roll (Difficulty 15) to identify the residue as characteristic of a shape-changing species, such as a Vespiform (essentially a giant wasp, not to be confused with a Wirrn – those are completely different!).

Characters looking for other signs of life in the alley may discover additional clues. An Awareness + Ingenuity roll (Difficulty 15) will turn up small buttons, ribbons or other pieces of cloth that suggest the ripping of clothes, probably accidentally left behind during quick trysts in the alleyway. This is known to be a popular spot for women of the night. It's likely that someone may have seen something when Terry left the theatre or when Wade came looking for her.

EDITH CRAIG

One of the reasons for concern for Terry's safety is that she lives with her daughter not far from the Lyceum, and she never came home last night. It's uncharacteristic for Terry to stay out late even when with someone else, and Edith was certain that Terry would have arrived home by midnight. Edith doesn't believe that her relationship with Shaw is anything but fellow professionals enjoying a correspondence and, having met the man, she believes him to be too timid to have tried something so bold.

Edith's brother, Edward, is also in the play but he is an extra and not presently at the theatre. He is married and lives apart, but Edith saw him this morning and he hadn't seen their mother either; he presumes that someone caught her fancy and she'll probably turn up sooner or later in the day.

THE MYSTERIOUS GENTLEMAN

Characters who ask appropriate questions, score a Fantastic Success on another investigative roll, or spend a Story Point, discover that at least one odd event took place early on in the show. In Act I, Terry was onstage as Guinevere when Irving arrived on stage as Arthur with his knights. A 'gentleman' wearing a long coat who'd purchased a ticket in the cheap seats worked his way down to the front of the stage and held his hat towards Terry. He stood there for a long minute, menacingly brushing away anyone who tried to get him to move. He finally relented and was escorted out of the theatre by an usher. The man seemed visibly relieved and almost excited as he apologised for the disturbance – some patrons thought they saw a slight green glow under his hat.

The description of the man makes him seem obviously of a lower class than he aspired to be; his clothes were threadbare and out of fashion. He had greasy light hair and smelled as if he hadn't had a bath in quite some time. His face was well-worn and he had a slight scar across the top of his forehead. This 'gentleman' is Adam Poole, and information about him can be found in **The Poole Gang** on pg. 106.

POSSIBLE DEDUCTION

While it may be a bit early for the characters to come to this conclusion, someone may deduce that the 'mysterious gentleman' may have been scanning for someone else and caught Ms Terry by mistake. This is exactly the case – he was actually scanning for Bethany Carter, who is secretly playing one of the male knights, but she is not due to arrive at the theatre until this evening.

If the characters think to ask if there is someone with similar features to Ms Terry, Ms Carter's name may pop up. As Carter is a patron and has asked to keep her ruse secret, discovering this information requires the right questions and a Presence + Convince roll (Difficulty 18) at this juncture. You may lower the difficulty if the characters make a convincing argument as to why there may be a connection.

2. POUNDING THE COBBLESTONES

Hopefully after visiting the Lyceum the characters have a few leads. These can be followed in any order and should hopefully lead to Benjamin 'Benny' Rumpole (the Vespiform) or Adam Poole (the scarred man). Alternatively, if the characters find themselves without any leads, however unlikely that may seem, they'll find their case suddenly closed by the mysterious reappearance of Ellen Terry!

THE STAGEHAND AND THE WASP

Even if the characters didn't discover the Vespiform Morphic residue in Burleigh Street, they still have two avenues left to discover it. The first is Malcolm Wade, the stagehand who Irving sent out to find Terry last night. The second are the 'Exeter Girls,' the ladies of easy virtue who frequent Exeter and Burleigh Streets to entertain patrons of the hall and the theatre. Malcolm Wade is currently drowning his sorrows in a pub near his Pimlico flat (an old regency-style home that's since been converted; the landlady, Ms Shield, points out that Wade seemed out of sorts at breakfast and mentioned something about needing a drink. Characters making an Awareness + Knowledge roll (Difficulty 12) find Wade at the Black Horse Pub only a couple streets away. Wade is drunk and doesn't want to talk about what happened – he's considering quitting the play. It takes a Presence + Convince roll (Difficulty 15) to get him to speak.

CUTTING TO THE CHASE?

Particularly devious players may stumble upon the idea of acquiring Ellen Terry's genetic signature and using that to find her. This might be done easily enough with a strand of hair from her hairbrush or – if the characters have reason to know about Irving's tryst – from his bedroom. If the characters can scan and locate Ellen Terry then they can solve the case rather quickly!

Whether you enable the characters to perform such a feat depends on the type of campaign you are fostering (see **The Art of Deduction, or Lack Thereof** on pg. 97), but note that enabling the characters to locate Ellen Terry quickly does not negate the greater mystery, which is *why* she was kidnapped – apparently erroneously – in the first place. Having spent most of the night unconscious, and hypnosis blocking out the one part she does remember, Terry probably won't give the characters enough clues to 'jump to the end' anyway!

Wade says that not long after the curtain call last night Mr Irving seemed positively furious. He sought Wade out because Wade had accepted the floral delivery for Ms Terry during the performance, although he didn't read the card. A Presence + Subterfuge roll (Difficulty 15) enables a character to determine that Wade is lying on this point; he was curious and read it. He tries to laugh it off if called on it, "you can't fault me for being curious" but tells them that the card only said "I've been admiring your beauty and have been entranced by your voice from the box for several nights now and tonight I am finally alone. I simply must see you. Please meet me at my blue carriage at the end of Burleigh Street towards Tavistock. With the utmost hope, Your Secret Admirer."

Wade didn't reveal this to Irving but there were other stagehands and actors who saw Terry's excitement before exiting out the back door: if her admirer had box seats then he was probably at least a gentleman and probably married; intriguing enough for Terry to at least see who it was. In any case, Wade was curious too and eagerly undertook Irving's demand that Wade find her. Wade rushed out the back door and looked for a blue carriage. He saw Terry struggling with some men, before being pushed inside the carriage! Wade chased after them and one of the men was dispatched to deal with him.

As a stagehand, Wade carries a large knife and, fearing for his person, he brandished it, hoping to scare off the attacker. Instead, the man lunged at him and Wade slashed the man's arm. That's when things got really strange; the man grunted and his features blurred and changed. Instead of a man, Wade was now facing a giant wasp! The wasp pointed its stinger at him but hesitated, so Wade turned and ran. He was bludgeoned in the back and went sprawling across the alley. He's unsure whether he blacked out but when he turned to face the wasp, it was gone! Fearing that he'd taken one too many 'nips' during the performance, he simply told Irving that he couldn't find her. After all, it was her own fault for going, right?

Wade still has the knife; he hasn't cleaned it because the 'blood' on it is brownish-yellow. A character who makes an Ingenuity + Medicine (or Science) roll (Difficulty 12) identifies it as alien, or Vespiform if the character or the gadget they are using would know such information.

The second avenue is talking to one of the women known to frequent the alley. This is a more challenging endeavour, but characters making a Presence + Knowledge roll (Difficulty 15) can eventually track down a suitable witness, Tilly Masters, at a flophouse on Holywell Street a couple of blocks away from the theatre. She's cautious about what she says – she doesn't want to be dragged to Bedlam – but if the characters can convince her to talk with a Presence + Convince roll (Difficulty 15) then she tells them that she was walking down Exeter Street when she heard a shriek and a noise from Burleigh Street (this was Wade). She turned the corner to see a "giant bee" ascending to the rooftops. She can tell them that it was heading in the general direction of Leper Hall (a short distance north-west of the theatre), if the characters think to ask that.

Once the characters discover that a Vespiform was involved in the disappearance they can take steps to find it. If the characters have access to a suitable gadget (or they make one using jiggery-pokery) then they can track the Vespiform's movements. While

there is only one Vespiform in London at the moment – Rumpole – tracking him isn't as easy as turning on the gadget. Rumpole's true form is hidden even from scanners while he is camouflaged.

Fortunately, there is one big clue. The Lyceum isn't far from Leper Hall and Rumpole flew back to it after being startled in the alleyway. He didn't bother returning to human form until he got to the roof of Leper Hall, so a pool of morphic residue remains on the roof of the building. More about investigation Leper Hall can be found in **The House of Me**, opposite.

THE POOLE GANG

The characters might also look into the Poole Gang. Discovering information about them requires a Presence + Knowledge roll (Difficulty 18). With a Success, the characters learn that Adam Poole, a labour union organiser, matches the description given for the mysterious gentleman at the theatre. With a Fantastic Success the characters learn that Poole operates out of Bermondsey and has a reputation for violence – while union leaders keep him at arm's length, they appreciate his ability to intimidate others. It is believed that he 'supplements' his income through various dubious and outright illegal activities.

With a Presence + Knowledge roll (Difficulty 15) the characters can discover that Poole can usually be found at his favourite watering hole, the Half Moon Pub, or his flat nearby in Bermondsey. Unfortunately for Poole and his gang (and any characters caught in the cross-fire), Professor Breen feels that they were too sloppy and is taking steps to eliminate them – see **Heist Clean-up** on pg. 108.

SIMILAR DISAPPEARANCES

At some point it may occur to the characters (perhaps if they spend a Story Point) that Ms Terry may have been taken for particular genetic characteristics; after all, the mysterious gentleman was scanning her with something before she disappeared! In this case, the characters need to discover all they can about her. The pertinent characteristics about Ms Terry are that she has flaxen (pale blonde) hair, grey eyes and is female – a very uncommon combination, but not exceedingly rare. There are roughly 15,000 women in London who fit the description (Scarlett Valentin fits this description too – a character who has met her in a previous adventure may recall that fact. See pg. 66 for more about Scarlett).

Characters who present this information to the police (or if they have a similar database of their own) can discover that several missing persons over the last three months fit the description. These missing persons came from all walks of life; the only thing they have in common – which can be discovered with an Ingenuity + Medicine or Science roll (Difficulty 15) or a Story Point – is that they are childless. The only person who breaks that mould is Ms Terry, which is why Scotland Yard rather blithely dismissed the connection. It didn't occur to them that someone might have made a mistake!

Obviously, this revelation might lead the characters to wonder if the wrong person was scanned at the play. While this is the case, a thorough examination of the actors and crew present yields no leads. The person in question is an extra, a knight without a speaking role played incognito by a woman. Edith Craig helpfully points out that this knight is Bethany Carter, a wealthy sponsor of the Lyceum who wanted a walk-on role with a minimum of fuss and thought it would be fun to dress up as a male character. She was humoured because of her generous donations and she was standing almost directly behind Ms Terry at the time she was scanned. Carter never married – she and Edith are actually in love – and is childless.

3. THE HOUSE OF ME

Characters following the clues left by the Vespiform invariably arrive at Leper Hall (see pg. 57 for a detailed description). If the characters look for information on Leper Hall then they need to make a Presence + Knowledge roll (Difficulty 12), which reveals it to be a hospital for lepers and other seriously ill people. A Fantastic Success garners juicier rumours: Leper Hall houses some very strange inhabitants, some of whom are believed to be well-versed in the magical arts and other preternatural phenomena.

There they are directed to Hester Biggs, the intimidating steward, who receives them in the grand

parlour. Alice, or Me, stands quietly in the next room, listening intently in on the conversation. Biggs warns them that this is a functioning hospital and that she needs to return to her duties as soon as possible, so whatever the characters want they should get right to the point. If the characters have met Me before then there is no charade; Me and Hester meet them together to inquire as to the reason for their visit.

If the characters play coy, then they get little in return from Hester. Should they badger her enough then she gets obviously upset and suggests that they leave; her disguise slips for a moment to reveal her true nature. If the characters mention that they are looking for a Vespiform then Hester gets extremely cross – her Judoon nature shows for a half-second – before angrily declaring that she'll need to have a talk with "Benny". At this point, Alice Shield, or Me, enters the room in a nurse's uniform and 'dismisses' Hester. This should be a shock to any character unfamiliar with Me, as she is obviously below her station!

JUDGE, JURY AND EXECUTIONER

Me orders Hester to find Mr Rumpole and bring him to the parlour. She then asks the characters if 'Benny' caused any trouble on the outside. Me runs a tight ship inside these walls, but she only restricts their activities if they threaten the integrity of Leper Hall or the timeline. Benny is a contemporary Vespiform, so any acts he causes won't threaten the timeline, but the characters' presence indicates that Benny is threatening the safety of Leper Hall. Unfortunately, that can't be tolerated and there is only one penalty for it – death. Hester arrives shortly with a very nervous Benjamin 'Benny' Rumpole, whom she practically shoves into the room. Me asks him directly what he's been up to and why these "pleasant investigators" have come looking for him. Benny talks fast, claiming that he had gotten into a spot of gambling trouble and was asked to participate in a job to pay off his debt. He didn't know that a kidnapping was involved until it was too late!

Me gives Benny a hard look and the Vespiform drops to his knees, begging her not to 'quit' him from the hall – he'd be happy to share any information. Behind him, Me tells him that she'd warned him about his gambling habits before and Benny knows the rules. Benny reverts to a quivering giant wasp as, behind him, Hester draws her blaster.

At this point, it's up to the characters to halt the execution. Me doesn't need too much convincing – this is largely for show and to frighten Benny into 'straightening up'; she realises that having the characters show up at her doorstep isn't as bad as Torchwood or even Scotland Yard (unless the characters work for those organisations instead!). It should be relatively easy for the characters to negotiate leniency in return for whomever Benny was paying off his debt to, or any other useful information.

Grateful to be alive, Benny tells all. He was playing in an unused warehouse in Bermondsey that acted as a gambling den operated by Adam Poole, but the location changes daily. In order to find the games, the characters either need to know someone or go to one of the pubs in Bermondsey, particularly the Half Moon, and ask the bartender if there is any room aboard "the Bombay". If the bartender thinks they are legitimate then he gives them a time and place. If he doesn't, then the characters had better watch their backs on the way out.

Benny participated in some games a few weeks ago and, after a blazing streak of good luck, fell hard. There was no way that he could pay off his gambling debt but Mr Poole offered him a clean slate if he participated in a little job for him. Benny eagerly accepted only to find that Poole would contact him when needed. Poole called in the debt last night and, before Benny knew what was happening, he was in a blue carriage on the way to kidnap someone. All Benny had to do was keep his mouth shut and ensure that no one followed.

Benny mentions that Poole kept mum about the exact nature of the kidnapping, only that his 'camera' would point out the target. Benny's description of the 'camera' marks it as some type of scanner, obviously cobbled together from local technology and using a single knob as an interface, so it's likely that Poole is in league with an alien – an alien other than Benny, of course.

Characters succeeding at an opposed Ingenuity + Convince roll opposed by Benny's Resolve + Convince (6) note that he isn't being entirely honest. He knows that if he'd gotten into too much trouble then he could have asked Me for assistance; Benny simply enjoys being a criminal. He was shocked that Poole picked such a high-profile target. If it looks like things are going bad for Benny, then he transforms into his Vespiform state and makes a desperate attack, but with Me and Hester aiding the characters he's unlikely to survive.

BENNY THE VESPIFORM

AWARENESS	3	PRESENCE	3
COORDINATION	3	RESOLVE	3
INGENUITY	2	STRENGTH	4

SKILLS
Athletics 2, Convince 3, Fighting 3, Knowledge 3, Marksman 2, Subterfuge 4, Survival 3, Technology 2, Transport 2.

TRAITS
Alien
Alien Appearance: In its natural form, the Vespiform looks like a giant wasp.
Keen Senses (Minor) – Sight: The Vespiform gains +2 to rolls when using its sight.
Natural Weapon – Stinger: The stinger is sharp, providing +4 to Strength in damage, but it also delivers a deadly poison that is usually lethal 4 (4/L/L) if the stinger does enough damage to penetrate any armour.
Shapeshift (Major): The Vespiform can appear as another form to blend into a planet's society. When angered or injured, it will usually transform back to its natural form.
Weakness: The Vespiform cannot swim and falling into water is fatal.

TECH LEVEL: 6 STORY POINTS: 2

4. HEIST CLEAN-UP

Characters who go looking for Adam Poole can either go to his flat or the Half Moon Pub – in the case of the former, residents there suggest the characters try the latter. The Half Moon is run by Billy Rakes, a rough-and-tumble sort who is one of Poole's old mates and the gatekeeper for Poole's gambling den. Assuming that the characters use the code phrase, they need only make a Presence + Convince roll (Difficulty 9) to persuade Rakes to give them the location of the latest game: the basement of a poor housing estate, the Guilfoyle, only a few streets away. Rakes warns them that "the ship doesn't leave for a couple of hours", meaning that the games aren't quite ready to start.

Regardless, that is exactly where Poole is at the moment. He is rather frantic, trying to get his game night together whilst discussing options with his men – four fellow ruffians – on whether they should return to the Lyceum and have another go. Poole is waiting on a couple of contacts that may know alternative possibilities for victims, since things are understandably hot for a return visit to the Lyceum.

NAPOLEONIC GAMBIT

Professor Breen is worried that Poole's failure will have attracted too much attention. She tried to hypnotise Poole but she doesn't think it worked. She shared her concern with Napoleon and the cunning Dalek has decided to take matters into his own hands, well, protuberances. He has ordered Miss Lovelace, over Mister Steele's objection, to "prove her worth" by analysing the situation and removing Poole at the most efficient opportunity.

Miss Lovelace has decided that it would be better to kill two birds with one stone and, for now, is observing the estate to see if any amateur sleuths, Scotland Yard detectives or other suspicious faces, visits Poole – obviously the characters fit the bill. Once that happens, Miss Lovelace orders an attack on the basement and leave no survivors.

Characters approaching the estate have a chance of spotting Miss Lovelace if they make an Awareness + Ingenuity roll (Difficulty 18). With a Success, they notice a pleasant, middle-class woman holding an umbrella (it's drizzling slightly) watching the estate. If the characters approach her then she puts her Cybershades on alert as she smiles at them, before walking away.

If the characters engage her then she tells them that she is simply on a stroll and found the architecture of the Guilfoyle Estate fascinating, especially its foundation. She then turns the question back on the characters, noting that they aren't local, and wondering what business they have on this street?

If the characters mention the gambling event then Lovelace pretends that she is a player too, waiting for the opening. For the most part, Miss Lovelace is charming but her words are laced with underlying menace. Adventurers making an Awareness + Ingenuity roll (Difficulty 15) – Keen Senses (Hearing) may be used on the roll – can hear the muffled whirring of clockwork beneath her dress.

If the characters scan her (except from a distance – Lovelace doesn't see them as a threat to her plans if they scan her but still go inside the estate) or otherwise engage her, Lovelace sighs and tells them that Poole's time is up. She then teleports to the basement and sends in her Cybershades, who have been lurking on the rooftops. Characters outside can, with an Awareness + Ingenuity roll (Difficulty 12), see them bounding towards the basement, shattering windows as they make various entrances for themselves. If the characters rush inside, then the fight is already in progress – skip to **Beauty and the Beasts**, overleaf.

POOLE PARTY

If the characters take the 'servant's entrance' into the basement they find themselves in a room with hastily placed tables and chairs. Poole is inside with four of his men, sitting around one of the tables and plotting his next move. Poole hears the characters open the door and waves them off, telling them that the games aren't due to start until 4 o'clock, unless they are here to discuss "flaxen" business (he believes they may be contacts with information regarding another blonde-haired, grey-eyed woman that may fit the requirements). Characters who play along may learn certain useful facts, including that Poole is looking for women with flaxen hair and grey eyes and that not everyone "fits the bill". The characters may even notice a bag nearby that contains his scanner.

If the characters mention the woman outside, then Poole brushes them off – she came earlier inquiring about the games. Poole told her – as he told them – that the games didn't start for a couple of hours. That seemed to satisfy her; she promised to return, glanced around a bit, and left. If the characters tell him that the woman is dangerous then Poole gets panicky – he knows that he is dealing with strange employers – and exclaims "no, they wouldn't! It was a simple mistake!"

The characters don't have much time before Lovelace strikes, but they can use an opposed Presence + Convince roll against Poole's Resolve + Convince (8) to make him reveal something before the Cybershades attack. With a Success, Poole reveals that he was hired to kidnap people with certain characteristics that "nobody would miss"; taking Ms Terry was a mistake. He's given much of his pay to various causes to ensure a network of people on the lookout for these characteristics – all blonde-haired, grey eyed women.

With a Good Success Poole tells them that his employer claimed that he misused the 'camera' and took the wrong woman, Ms Terry. His employer 'mesmerised' Terry into forgetting what she saw and put her to sleep – Poole thinks she tried to do something similar to him but backed off when he begged for a chance to set things right (in truth, Breen's hypnotism didn't work on Poole due to his Indomitable trait). She told him that she'd "fix everything" but something about her tone didn't sit well with him.

With a Fantastic Success, the characters gain two additional pieces of information from Poole. The first is that Ellen Terry was left in the blue carriage in Hammersmith, where hopefully she'll wake up and remember nothing, and that Poole's employer is also a woman who fits the profile; she goes by the name of Professor Breen and she operates out of an old warehouse on the Isle of Dogs that Poole helped arrange for her. She always seems sick, but Poole believes she has powerful friends; he waited all night for her at the warehouse until she returned from a visit with one of those "friends" early this morning. Poole doesn't remember how she arrived – he heard a strange noise in her "Engine Room" and she emerged from it – she must've snuck in through a window or something. No one bothers exploring Breen's Engine Room because of her strange-looking, highly trained dogs.

BEAUTY AND THE BEASTS

Unfortunately, the characters won't have long to speak with Poole – if they have any time at all – because Lovelace and her 'pets' soon strike. Four Cybershades smash into the room and begin attacking Poole, his gang and anyone else in the room (which should just be the characters, unless they've brought someone). After the first round, Miss Lovelace teleports inside as well, guarding the side entrance so no one else escapes.

Poole doesn't recognise Lovelace and, in spite of being in mortal danger, demands to know who she is. Lovelace simply smiles and says that she is the housemaid, cleaning up after a particularly troublesome mess. She isn't afraid to get her hands dirty and doesn't hesitate to attack if the opportunity affords itself. She certainly wants Poole dead and to retrieve his scanner, but if the battle goes poorly then she'll conserve resources by pulling back, content to report in to Napoleon to get new orders.

If the characters manage to save Poole (or at least one of his men) then he can supply them with the addresses of where Terry was left as well as the warehouse Breen is using. Poole also tells them that Breen keeps her part of the warehouse guarded – he and his men keep to the loading entrance area when bringing new victims.

ARTRON ECHOES

A character will have to take the device apart to determine its purpose, then make an Ingenuity + Science roll (Difficulty 15). With at least a Failure the character can tell that someone experienced with early 51st century Earth technology put this together, but it's still slightly primitive for a Time Agent. With a Success, the character determines that the scanner measures Artron energy. With a good result the character discovers the scanner's true purpose: it measures Artron 'echoes'; or how strongly a being's life affects the future; specifically 51st century. In other words, it determines how integral a person's life is to the timeline and whether ending such a life prematurely would have more than a minimal impact.

NEW GADGET – ARTRON SCANNER (MINOR GADGET)

The scanner has a very basic function. The front of it has a single scanning lens. There is a toggle for on and off and two small lights; one red, one green, on the back. The device is designed to detect Artron energy, specifically Artron echoes.

Traits: Scan, Restriction (Artron energy only)
Story Points: 1

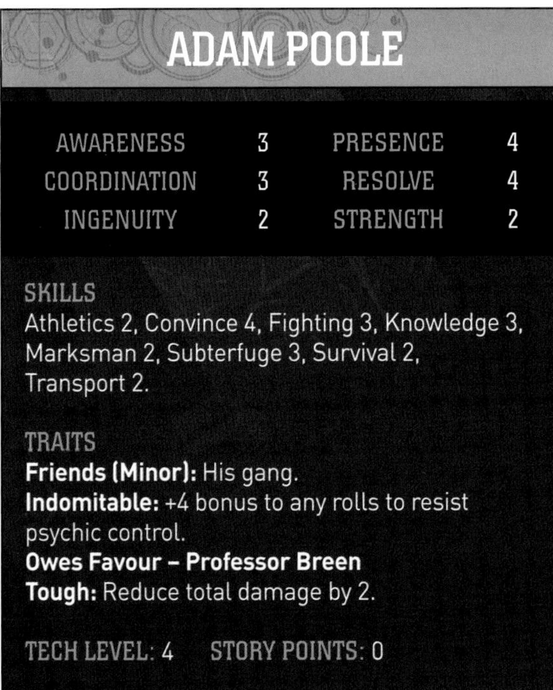

ADAM POOLE

AWARENESS	3	PRESENCE	4
COORDINATION	3	RESOLVE	4
INGENUITY	2	STRENGTH	2

SKILLS
Athletics 2, Convince 4, Fighting 3, Knowledge 3, Marksman 2, Subterfuge 3, Survival 2, Transport 2.

TRAITS
Friends (Minor): His gang.
Indomitable: +4 bonus to any rolls to resist psychic control.
Owes Favour – Professor Breen
Tough: Reduce total damage by 2.

TECH LEVEL: 4 STORY POINTS: 0

POOLE'S RUFFIANS

AWARENESS	2	PRESENCE	2
COORDINATION	3	RESOLVE	2
INGENUITY	1	STRENGTH	3

SKILLS
Athletics 2, Fighting 2, Marksman 1, Transport 1.

TRAITS
Tough (Minor Good): Reduce total damage by 2.

TECH LEVEL: 4 STORY POINTS: 0

5. CASE UNEXPECTEDLY CLOSED?

If the characters discovered Ellen Terry's whereabouts from Adam Poole, then they will find her still passed out, unconscious (thanks to a healthy inhalation of chloroform), in a blue carriage left in an alley in Hammersmith. She's no worse for wear except for a strong smell of alcohol (Poole liberally doused her clothes and the carriage with alcohol) and a dishevelled appearance – she looks as though she had a fun night on the town but it got the better of her.

In spite of Terry's appearance, a character using any type of medical scanner can, with an Ingenuity + Medicine roll (Difficulty 9), determine that she wasn't drunk. There were, however, traces of chloroform in her system.

If the characters dally in locating her (she wakes up mid-morning), then they instead find the empty carriage. A quick canvassing of the neighbourhood will, with a Presence + Convince roll (Difficulty 18), discover that a confused woman was seen wandering the street earlier but she managed to convince a hansom driver to take her somewhere (she's on her way back to the Lyceum).

LUNCHEON SURPRISE

If the characters fail to discover Terry's whereabouts, something very unexpected happens just after lunch: Ellen Terry is found, alive and well! She stumbled out of a blue carriage (the same one that abducted her) in an alley in Hammersmith, with no recollection of the previous night. Her clothes smell of spirits and she was only able to hire a cab to take her to the Lyceum on the strength of her reputation and a promise that

Henry Irving would pay the fare. Irving was delighted to see her – albeit suspicious of the circumstances – and sent word to the police. The police, in turn, send word to the characters (or their employer, if the characters don't have a direct connection to Scotland Yard).

A MATTER OF MEMORY

If the characters interview Terry, they discover that she remembers nothing after leaving the Lyceum and spending a fun evening with 'Bernie' (George Bernard Shaw). If pressed, she gets increasingly agitated as she realises that she can't recall anything specific, just that she had a fun time and can't wait to see him again.

A character who makes an Ingenuity + Medicine roll (Difficulty 15), or who has the Hypnosis trait at any level, can tell that Terry has been hypnotised. Whilst this is an obstacle, it's one that, if overcome, can provide the characters with the final piece in the puzzle. Her information about where she's been is still buried deeply in her mind; all the characters have to do is coax her out of it.

How the characters accomplish this is up to them. While Terry is under the influence, the battle is actually played out between Fiora Breen and the character trying to break the conditioning. This is a lot like Possession (see the **Doctor Who Roleplaying Game**), except that it is Breen's Presence + Convince + Technology used (for a total of 9) against the character's Presence + Convince (and perhaps a bonus if the character has access to an appropriate gadget).

With a Success, Terry recalls that she was kidnapped by ruffians (Poole's gang) and had something put over her mouth, and then she fell unconscious. She remembers being awake and somewhere on the docks of East London and a woman's voice telling her to forget everything but being with Mr Shaw. She then fell unconscious again after a flash from a strange dog. With a Good Success, Terry remembers the woman's face – middle-aged and with fierce grey eyes (if asked, Terry confirms that her hair was blonde as well). She also remembers that there was something wrong with her; the woman seemed feverish and had scars on her face like she'd suffered burns in the past.

Even with a regular Success, the characters can bring Terry along to jog her memory as to the warehouse location if the information has not been obtained from Poole. At any rate, the characters soon find themselves at Breen's warehouse on the Isle of Dogs.

6. TEMPORAL WORKSHOP

Professor Breen operates out of a warehouse on the Isle of Dogs. She has cannibalised her Time Cabinet to create a teleporter between her warehouse and Dr Karfelov's castle. This teleporter is largely based on

Dalek Time Corridor technology but, as yet, Breen has only made it work as a matter transporter between the two machines – it is not capable of time travel. Furthermore, Breen can only run the machine once every few days because of its vast power consumption and, when she uses it, it takes its toll on her genetically damaged body.

From the outside, the warehouse looks little different than any other. The exterior doors aren't even locked (Breen relies on her 'dogs' to stun unwelcome intruders so that she can hypnotise them to leave and forget about it. The main room looks as if it's been abandoned for years with makeshift tables and chairs constructed from old crates. The only other room in the place is the Engine Room, within which frequent hissing and humming can be heard. Normally, the Ryukyu guardians sit in here, ready to stun anyone who enters and attack should they try to access the Engine Room.

The Engine Room is locked with a fairly sophisticated optical lock of 51st century design (cannibalised from the Time Cabinet). It is notoriously difficult to pick, requiring an Ingenuity + Technology roll (Difficulty 21). It's probably easier to cut through the iron door.

Depending on how the fight is going, Professor Breen either activates TS-1953 and joins the fight (presuming the dogs are doing well) or she simply waits in the Engine Room to deal with the characters after they've been softened up.

THE ENGINE ROOM

'The Engine Room' should be more properly called 'the Engines Room' given that it houses no less than three machines (if one doesn't count TS-1953). The first is Professor Breen's Time Cabinet, a primitive time machine that uses dangerous Zygma Beams to punch holes through time and space. Breen's model is an 8-foot cube that managed to hold Breen, two lion-dogs and a spherical robot. Unfortunately, it is currently quite useless, as Breen has cannibalised it for her other machines.

The second machine is an ironically named 'Genetic Stabiliser,' which is basically two coffins held together with machinery. Breen operates it by placing a victim in one coffin and clambering into the other herself. Once the transfer of life force is made, the victim dies, leaving only a dried out husk that is pitched into the Thames through a trapdoor in the floor.

The third machine actually sits above the Engine Room and is accessible by a staircase that winds around its spherical hull, with a variety of 19th century machinery retooled to approximate future technology attached to the hull. Inside is the mirror room, which is lined with mirrors. This 'Time Conduit' is a hodgepodge of various time travel technologies; it contains elements of Breen's Time Cabinet, Dalek Time Corridor technology and Dr Karfelov's recollection of the schematics of the Timelash. All of these have been reworked into Victorian inventors' Theodore Maxtible and Edward Waterfield's successful time machine, which Napoleon has copied from his memory archives of the project.

Understanding that the game is up, Professor Breen tries to appeal to the characters' logic and pity. She explains that she is only doing what she has to do, for if she doesn't return to her own time and warn the rest of her team about the folly of Zygma Beams then it is only a matter of time before someone else takes a trip and threatens to rip the world apart. This is only partially true; Breen's own professional pride is getting in the way, as she was certain that she'd fixed the problems with the Time Cabinets. She can't let her legacy stand as it is.

Unfortunately, there is probably little that the characters can do if they parley. Breen is absolutely convinced that her work must continue unabated and for that she needs more victims. She can't trust the characters to keep their word; she'll go to Napoleon at the earliest opportunity to 'remove' them.

If the characters put up a fight, Breen hopes that the TS-1953 and her stun pistol can keep them at bay. Should the battle go poorly, then Professor Breen retreats. She runs up the staircase and throws a switch, intending to travel to Dr Karfelov's castle. Unfortunately, the Borad is already listening and watching through the mirrors...

BETRAYED!

Unless Breen successfully incapacitates the characters, then Dr Karfelov decides that she has become a liability. He orders Josephine (see pg. 75) to overload the machine and the mirrors shatter in hisses of steam – anyone caught inside the mirror room takes 3/7/10 levels of damage. If Breen is inside, then she is killed. The Borad maintains this trap even if Breen is incapacitated so that anyone trying to get through suffers the same fate.

If anyone is inside the mirror room with Breen, an Awareness + Ingenuity roll (Difficulty 12) allows them to see an image in one of the mirrors, a creature's

RYUKYU GUARDIANS

AWARENESS	3	PRESENCE	2
COORDINATION	5	RESOLVE	5
INGENUITY	1	STRENGTH	3

The Ryukyu Guardians are a pair of robotic dogs with leonine features that have had canine brains implanted in them. They were created at the behest of Magnus Greel to protect strategic locations for the Icelandic Alliance and, after the alliance fell, many of these cybernetic 'lion-dogs' remained in use. Two were assigned to accompany Breen in her Time Cabinet in case she met trouble in the past. Breen now uses them to protect her Engine Room from prying eyes.

SKILLS
Athletics 3, Fighting 4.

TRAITS
Cyborg
Armour: Reduce damage by 5.
Fear Factor (2): Grants a +4 bonus to inspire fear.
Natural Weapons – Teeth and Claws: Close combat weapons that do 2/5/7 levels of damage.
Natural Weapons – Stun Blast: A ranged weapon that does Stun (S/S/S) damage.
Weakness (Special): Pulling the fuse from the cyborg's back (with a Coordination + Fighting test against the creature) turns it off.

TECH LEVEL: 8 STORY POINTS: 3

TS-1953

AWARENESS	3	PRESENCE	1
COORDINATION	3	RESOLVE	3
INGENUITY	1	STRENGTH	4

The TS-1953 is a security robot of late 50th century design. It is a small sphere, about the size of a football, that either walks on three legs or, more commonly, retracts the legs so that the tips emanate anti-gravity beams for 'flight.' A TS-1953 is coded to accept commands only from authorised commanders. Overriding this encryption requires a tool – such as a Sonic Screwdriver – and an Ingenuity + Technology roll (Difficulty 18).

SKILLS
Fighting 2, Marksman 4.

TRAITS
Alien Senses: The TS-1953 gets a +4 to Awareness when using thermal vision.
Armour (5): The TS-1953 has a reinforced shell. Reduce damage by 5.
Flight (Minor): The TS-1953 can hover at up to 100 metres and fly at half its speed.
Natural Weapons – Laser Gun Stick: The TS-1953 is armed with a laser gun stick that does Stun (S/S/S) or Lethal (4/L/L) damage.
Robot

TECH LEVEL: 8 STORY POINTS: 3

face that looks half-man and half-reptile (the Borad). The creature seems to be either sneering or laughing at them! After the explosion, Breen, with her dying breath, begs the characters to stop "Napoleon and the..." before she trails off and dies.

ENDING THE ADVENTURE

After the characters have defeated Breen and stepped back out onto the docks they may, with an Awareness + Ingenuity roll (Difficulty 15), notice Miss Lovelace standing on a neighbouring pier, quietly watching them (if the characters managed to dispatch her earlier then will be Mister Steele instead). She disappears before the characters can approach her, perhaps leaving them with the impression that Napoleon was behind Breen's betrayal. That is not the case – Miss Lovelace is observing them and Napoleon will be troubled by this development – as he is questioning the Borad's loyalty for himself.

For now, however, the characters are heroes. They've solved the mystery of Ellen Terry's disappearance and prevented other women from suffering an ugly fate. Scotland Yard is happy to clean up the mess, although the Borad has already alerted the Torchwood Institute and their agents will swoop in to pick up the interesting pieces of technology. There are a number of leads left hanging – Napoleon and the Borad remain at large, of course – at the conclusion of the adventure. The perfect jumping off point for the Paternoster Gang's next investigation!

PROFESSOR FIORA BREEN

Professor Breen is a temporal engineer from the 51st century. She is trying to perfect Time Cabinet technology, but has run afoul of the same problems with the Zygma Beams as the last time traveller, Magnus Greel. Due to the limitations of the technology she has landed roughly in the same time a few years later and she too is undergoing genetic decay. She has been stabilising herself by absorbing the life force from close genetic matches, but her quest to perfect her machine continues to expose her to more Zygma energy.

AWARENESS	3	PRESENCE	4/3*
COORDINATION	3/2*	RESOLVE	4
INGENUITY	5/4*	STRENGTH	3/2*

*Breen's reduced attributes are the result of genetic deterioration. If she drains a compatible victim she regains 1D6+1 attribute points (until she reaches her maximum – any excess is lost).

SKILLS

Convince 3, Craft 4, Fighting 1, Knowledge 5, Marksman 3, Medicine 2, Science 3 (Temporal Physics 5), Survival 2, Technology 3 (Temporal Technology 5), Transport 3 (Time Machine 5).

TRAITS

Boffin: Breen can create Gadgets.
Code of Conduct (Minor): Breen is extremely careful not to create big ripples in the timeline. She prefers to incapacitate rather than kill.
Distinctive: Breen's genetic condition gives her a -2 penalty to rolls to blend in. Others have a +2 bonus to remember or recognise her.
Fear Factor (1): Breen's condition and her anachronistic technology provides her with a +2 bonus to inspire fear.
Hypnosis (Major): Breen is trained in hypnosis and gets a +2 bonus to control another's actions and feelings.
Owes Favour (Major): Breen is indebted to Dr Karfelov and, by extension, Napoleon.
Obsession (Major): Breen's arrogance and pride refuses to let her abandon the project – she will either get home or die in the process.
Technically Adept: Breen gets a +2 to any Technology roll to fix a broken or faulty device.
Time Traveller (Minor): Breen is familiar with Tech Level 4.
Vortex: Breen may pilot time craft through the Vortex, and gains +2 when doing so.
Weakness (Major): Travelling through time or teleportation inflicts 4 levels of damage to Breen because of her unstable genes. In addition, Breen's genetic damage means that she also takes 1 point of damage per day.

EQUIPMENT

Partially-operational Time Cabinet, Stun Pistol (S/S/S damage), Hypnosis Clock (adds +2 to hypnotism effects).

TECH LEVEL: 8 STORY POINTS: 9

APPENDIX: CHARACTER SHEETS

BBC DOCTOR WHO ROLEPLAYING GAME

MADAME VASTRA

STORY POINTS 6

ATTRIBUTES

AWARENESS	4
COORDINATION	4
INGENUITY	5
PRESENCE	4
RESOLVE	4
STRENGTH	5

SKILLS

Skill	Score	Skill	Score
ATHLETICS	3	MEDICINE	2
CONVINCE	3	SCIENCE	3
CRAFT	0	SUBTERFUGE (Disguise 5)	3
FIGHTING	4	SURVIVAL	3
KNOWLEDGE	4	TECHNOLOGY	3
MARKSMAN (Tongue 5)	3	TRANSPORT	1

BIODATA

PERSONAL GOAL

To solve mysteries, uncover secrets, and stand against all dangers.

PERSONALITY

Vastra is a mighty warrior, but her chief weapon is her mind. She is a skilled and insightful detective and draws great satisfaction from her successes. She is open-minded and delights in defying convention, and she has even found love for a human. Nevertheless, she is a reptile, not a mammal, and she has a streak of ruthlessness that she does not keep hidden.

BACKGROUND

Vastra awoke from hibernation in the early 1880s and in a rage she killed several Underground workers in vengeance for the deaths of her sisters. The Doctor put her on a new path, protectress of London and humanity. Vastra set up house at 13 Paternoster Row, making herself available to aid Scotland Yard and also private individuals facing vexing mysteries. Her maidservant Jenny Flint became her investigative companion, then her lover, then her wife, giving clear proof of how far her views on humanity had changed since she awoke. Vastra has repaid the Doctor many times over, helping him at Demon's Run and protecting him when he was in hiding or in a state of post-regenerative confusion.

TRAITS

Alien
Armour (Minor, 5)
Brave
Environmental: Extreme heat
Friends (Major, The Doctor)
Friends (Minor, Paternoster Gang)
Friends (Minor, Paternoster Irregulars)
Keen Senses (Major)
Quick Reflexes
Agent of Scotland Yard
Social Class (Upper)
Special – Tongue Attack*
Telepathy (with Jenny only)
Time Traveller (Minor, Tech Level 4)

*Tongue - Range 3m, S/S/S or mutation venom (Strength + Resolve, diff. 12, every hour or mutate)

Alien Appearance (Major)
Code of Conduct (doesn't kill humans)
Dark Secret (Eats People)
Last of My Kind
Weakness (Minor, Cold)
Weakness (Major, Hexachromite Gas)

STUFF

Mask or veil
Katana (4/8/12)

6

BBC DOCTOR WHO ROLEPLAYING GAME

JENNY FLINT

STORY POINTS 12

ATTRIBUTES

3	AWARENESS
4	COORDINATION
4	INGENUITY
3	PRESENCE
5	RESOLVE
3	STRENGTH

SKILLS

Value	Skill	Value	Skill
3	ATHLETICS	2	MEDICINE
3	CONVINCE	2	SCIENCE
2	CRAFT	4	SUBTERFUGE
4	FIGHTING	3	SURVIVAL
3	KNOWLEDGE	2	TECHNOLOGY
2	MARKSMAN	2	TRANSPORT

BIODATA

PERSONAL GOAL

To protect the vulnerable and root out evil wherever it may hide. All in a day's work!

PERSONALITY

Jenny is quiet and reserved, but she has a fiercely open mind and a taste for adventure that defies both her sex and her class. Also, she married another woman, and a reptilian one at that. Jenny understands the importance of keeping up appearances but will not allow conventional expectations to limit her life or her choices.

BACKGROUND

Born in London's East End to an impoverished school teacher, Jenny became the trusted companion of the mysterious consulting detective Madame Vastra. Her life became full of adventure and wonder. She rose to every challenge put before her and won Vastra's respect and admiration, and eventually her love. She and Vastra are married, although Jenny still plays housemaid in their daily life.

TRAITS

Brave
Empathic
Friends (Major, The Doctor)
Friends (Minor, Paternoster Gang)
Friends (Minor, Paternoster Irregulars)
Keen Senses (Major, All senses)
Quick Reflexes
Telepathy (with Vastra only)
Time Traveller (Minor, Tech Level 4)

Obligation (Major, Protect Madame Vastra)

STUFF

Leather fighting uniform (Armour 1)
Sword (3/7/10)
Scanner glove (Minor Gadget, Trait: Scan, Story Points: 1)

4

STRAX

STORY POINTS 8

ATTRIBUTES

AWARENESS	3
COORDINATION	4
INGENUITY	3
PRESENCE	4
RESOLVE	6
STRENGTH	6

SKILLS

Skill	Value	Skill	Value
ATHLETICS	3	MEDICINE	4
CONVINCE	1	SCIENCE	3
CRAFT	0	SUBTERFUGE	3
FIGHTING	5	SURVIVAL	4
KNOWLEDGE (War 5)	3	TECHNOLOGY	3
MARKSMAN	5	TRANSPORT	3

BIODATA

PERSONAL GOAL
Strax always does his duty, especially when his duty involves his enormous skill at warfare.

PERSONALITY
Strax is driven to excel in battle, and where that fails he'll do his best to be a good butler, or cab driver, or nurse. His experiences have made him a very unusual Sontaran, and he feels something like friendship for his current commanding officer Madame Vastra and the human scum who serve with him. He now positively enjoys protecting weaklings who would die quickly in any proper war.

BACKGROUND
After his clone batch was defeated by the Doctor, Strax pledged to regain his honour by becoming a nurse. Eventually the Doctor asked him to help in the battle at Demon's Run, where he met Madame Vastra and Jenny Flint. After they saved his life, he joined them as their butler, coach driver and chief military adviser. He has followed their orders, and offered plenty of much-needed tactical advice, ever since.

TRAITS

Alien
Brave
Friends (Major): The Doctor
Friends (Minor): Paternoster Gang
Friends (Minor, Paternoster Irregulars)
Tough

Alien Appearance (Minor)
By the Book
Eccentric
Know your Place
Obligation (Major): The Doctor
Special – Probic Vent *(a hit to the vent will stun Strax; -4 penalty on attempts to target the vent)*
Weakness (Major, Coronic Acid)

STUFF

Sontaran Rifle (4/L/L)
Shock Staff (S/S/S)
Battle armour (5)
Medical scanner (Minor Gadget; Trait: Scan, Story Points: 1)

7

BBC
DOCTOR WHO
ROLEPLAYING GAME

JACKSON LAKE

STORY POINTS 12

ATTRIBUTES

Attribute	Value
AWARENESS	3
COORDINATION	3
INGENUITY	5
PRESENCE	4
RESOLVE	4
STRENGTH	3

SKILLS

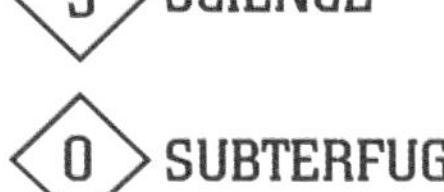

Skill	Value	Skill	Value
ATHLETICS	3	MEDICINE	0
CONVINCE	3	SCIENCE	5
CRAFT	4	SUBTERFUGE	0
FIGHTING	2	SURVIVAL	0
KNOWLEDGE	5	TECHNOLOGY	3
MARKSMAN	0	TRANSPORT	3

BIODATA

PERSONAL GOAL

To run from his past and embrace the future he believes is his.

PERSONALITY

There are two men in Jackson Lake's mind. The first is the Doctor; an endlessly confident, flamboyant scientist-adventurer who battles evil. Then there's the grieving, traumatised widower, unable to face what happened to his wife and his son. He throws himself headlong into his belief that he is the Doctor; desperate, ebullient and terrified. The (real) Doctor helps him become himself again: a brave, kind father who will do anything to save his son.

BACKGROUND

Jackson met the Doctor shortly after Jackson's wife had been killed by Cybermen. Using an Infostamp containing information on the Doctor to defend himself, Jackson absorbed its memories and believed he was the Doctor. With the Doctor's help, Jackson realised the truth and saved his son. With Jackson's help, the Doctor saved London from Miss Hartigan and the Cybermen.

TRAITS

Boffin
Brave
Code of Conduct
Imprinted Memories
Indomitable
Person of Repute
Resourceful Pockets
Technically Adept

Adversary (Cybermen)
Amnesia (Major)
Dark Secret *(Blames himself for his wife's death)*
Impulsive

STUFF

Sonic Screwdriver (well, all right then, it's an ordinary screwdriver)

4

ROSITA FARISI

STORY POINTS 12

ATTRIBUTES

3	AWARENESS
3	COORDINATION
5	INGENUITY
3	PRESENCE
5	RESOLVE
4	STRENGTH

SKILLS

Value	Skill	Value	Skill
4	ATHLETICS	0	MEDICINE
4	CONVINCE	0	SCIENCE
0	CRAFT	0	SUBTERFUGE
3	FIGHTING	3	SURVIVAL
4	KNOWLEDGE	0	TECHNOLOGY
0	MARKSMAN	0	TRANSPORT

BIODATA

PERSONAL GOAL
To find a decent place for herself in life.

PERSONALITY
Rosita is a straight talker. She is always polite, but doesn't mince her words, whether facing injustice or hundred-foot tall Cybermen. She has a strong sense of personal honour and does not forget a debt, especially the one she owes Jackson Lake for saving her life.

BACKGROUND
Brought up on the street, Rosita saw very little future for herself. But then she met the Doctor and everything changed. Even though the Doctor turned out not to be the Doctor at all, but a funny gentleman who was having something of a turn, he proved to be a good friend. Given that Jackson needs a bit of looking after, Rosita has become his companion.

TRAITS

Brave
Quick Reflexes
Screamer!

Code of Conduct

STUFF

None

4

BBC DOCTOR WHO ROLEPLAYING GAME

HENRY GORDON JAGO

STORY POINTS 10

ATTRIBUTES

Attribute	Value
AWARENESS	2
COORDINATION	2
INGENUITY	3
PRESENCE	4
RESOLVE	3
STRENGTH	2

SKILLS

Skill	Value	Skill	Value
ATHLETICS	0	MEDICINE	0
CONVINCE (Oratory 5)	3	SCIENCE	0
CRAFT	0	SUBTERFUGE	2
FIGHTING	1	SURVIVAL	0
KNOWLEDGE	4	TECHNOLOGY	1
MARKSMAN	1	TRANSPORT	1

BIODATA

PERSONAL GOAL

To have a magnificent idea to make his fortune.

PERSONALITY

Jago would be at home as a carnival sideshow hustler. He is polite but a little brash, and often the loudest voice at the dinner table. He is constantly on the lookout for 'the next big thing', hoping that he will be the one to make a fortune from it. However, even though he yearns to be rich, he is both generous and something of a gambler, understanding that you need to spend money to make money.

BACKGROUND

Jago has built his fortune in true middle class fashion. The theatre he has come to own may not be the best, but it is a tidy investment. While it takes all his time to fill the bill and provide his audience with new acts, he loves the hustle and bustle of theatre life. His encounter with the Doctor inspired in him a new sense of adventure, even if he also hopes it will lead to riches.

TRAITS

Charming
Empathic
Lucky

Eccentric (Minor): *Why use one short word when five long words will do!*
Impulsive
Insatiable Curiosity
Obsession (Minor Bad): *Jago is always looking out for new ways to make his fortune.*

STUFF

None

4

BBC DOCTOR WHO ROLEPLAYING GAME

PROFESSOR LITEFOOT

STORY POINTS 10

ATTRIBUTES

3	AWARENESS
2	COORDINATION
5	INGENUITY
2	PRESENCE
3	RESOLVE
2	STRENGTH

SKILLS

Value	Skill	Value	Skill
2	ATHLETICS	5	MEDICINE
2	CONVINCE	4	SCIENCE
0	CRAFT	0	SUBTERFUGE
1	FIGHTING	0	SURVIVAL
4	KNOWLEDGE	1	TECHNOLOGY
2	MARKSMAN	1	TRANSPORT

BIODATA

PERSONAL GOAL

To understand the mysteries that science can reveal.

PERSONALITY

Litefoot is first and foremost an Englishman. He remains polite and well-mannered no matter what the situation, or who is pointing a gun at him. It's not just the way he was brought up, it's simply the right way to behave. While he doesn't really like adventure, he cannot resist a good mystery. A puzzle for the mind is always the most fascinating challenge for him. If he is needed he will always answer the call.

BACKGROUND

Litefoot spent most of his childhood in China with his family. Unlike a lot of colonials, he took an interest in Chinese culture and tradition and came to understand both very well indeed. Returning to England he pursued a career in academia. This led him to police work as a forensic advisor, which suited his taste for a good mystery.

TRAITS

Brave
Charming
Agent of Scotland Yard
Insatiable Curiosity
Lucky
Person of Repute

Code of Conduct (Minor Bad): *Litefoot always behaves like a gentleman, especially with ladies present.*

STUFF

Medical kit

4

BBC DOCTOR WHO ROLEPLAYING GAME

CLARA OSWIN OSWALD

STORY POINTS 12

ATTRIBUTES

Score	Attribute
3	AWARENESS
3	COORDINATION
4	INGENUITY
3	PRESENCE
4	RESOLVE
2	STRENGTH

SKILLS

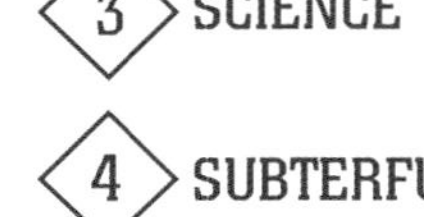

Score	Skill	Score	Skill
3	ATHLETICS	0	MEDICINE
4	CONVINCE	3	SCIENCE
2	CRAFT	4	SUBTERFUGE
2	FIGHTING	1	SURVIVAL
4	KNOWLEDGE (History 6)	3	TECHNOLOGY
2	MARKSMAN	3	TRANSPORT

BIODATA

PERSONAL GOAL

To help innocent people in trouble.

PERSONALITY

Clara is happy, energetic and whip-smart. She is forthright and likes to take control of any situation. She considers the Doctor her most trusted friend, and would sacrifice herself to save him. (She's already done it once.) She has matured and become more confident through her travels with the Doctor, and senses the value of maintaining a strong grounded ordinary life rather than disappearing entirely into the Doctor's world.

BACKGROUND

To the working classes, Clara is a young woman who can often be found helping out at the Rose and Crown pub in the East End. To the Latimer children, she is Miss Montegue, a slightly prim governess who has a way with children. To the Paternoster Gang and the Doctor, she is a splinter of Clara Oswald, in Victorian London to save the Doctor's timeline from the Great Intelligence.

TRAITS

Attractive
Brave
Friends (Major – the Doctor)
Indomitable
Keen Senses (Major)
Lucky

Eccentric
Insatiable Curiosity

STUFF

None

BBC
DOCTOR WHO ROLEPLAYING GAME

VICTORIA WATERFIELD

STORY POINTS 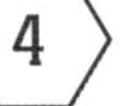 12

ATTRIBUTES

Level	Attribute
3	AWARENESS
3	COORDINATION
2	INGENUITY
4	PRESENCE
4	RESOLVE
2	STRENGTH

SKILLS

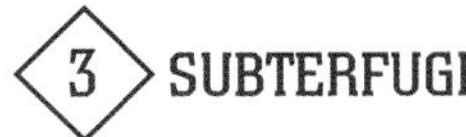

Level	Skill	Level	Skill
1	ATHLETICS	1	MEDICINE
3	CONVINCE	3	SCIENCE
0	CRAFT	3	SUBTERFUGE
1	FIGHTING	1	SURVIVAL
2	KNOWLEDGE	2	TECHNOLOGY
2	MARKSMAN	1	TRANSPORT

BIODATA

PERSONAL GOAL
To find a stable lifestyle again.

PERSONALITY
Victoria is a bit shy and timid. While no coward, she does have a tendency to scream at the first sign of trouble. She can hold her own in an argument, provided it remains cordial.

BACKGROUND
Victoria is a Victorian young lady forced to travel with the Doctor rather than be left on Skaro after her father's death. While she enjoys travelling with the Doctor and Jamie, she really longs to return to a simpler life.

TRAITS

Attractive
Charming
Empathic
Impulsive
Screamer!
Time Traveller (Minor): Victoria learns to adapt to Tech Level 5 during her travels with the Doctor.

Code of Conduct: *Victoria has the prim and proper attitude and values of a Victorian woman raised in a middle class home.*
Unadventurous

STUFF

Victoria doesn't tend to travel with much, although she carries a bag on occasion.

Note: Victoria's Subterfuge skill applies only to lock-picking.

INDEX

1887 – The Golden Jubilee 21
1888 – A City Gripped by Fear 22
1889 – Strikes and Scandals 23
1891 – Technology Marches On 24
1893 – Piercing the Veil 25
1895 – The Time Machine 26
1897 – Preternatural Fact and Fiction 26
1898 – The War of the Worlds 28

A
Academic 80
(The) Adventurer's Society 41
Adventures in Central London 37
Adventures in East London 39
Adventures in North London 44
Adventures in South London 42
Adventures in West London 40
Adventures in the Victorian Age 31
(An) Age of Marvels 7
Alien Characters 82
Alien Mindsets 19
Alien Refugees 79
Aliens in London 96
(The) Ale Society 43
(Elizabeth Garrett) Anderson 15
(Miss) Annie 56
(Mary) Anning 14
(The) Andromeda Club 41
Army Officer 80
(The) Art of Deduction, or Lack Thereof 97
(The) Artful Dodger 55
Artists 11
(Rhona) Austen 72

B
(Charles) Babbage 13
(Professor Augusta) Barlow 46
Benny the Vespiform 108
(The) Bethlehem Royal Hospital 43
(Hester) Biggs 59
(Isabella) Bird 14
(The) Birth of the Great Detective 20
(Nurse Janet) Blackwood 47
(The) Blizzard 24
(A) Bluffer' Guide to Parliament 36
(The) Borad 73
(Professor Fiona) Breen 115
(Isambard Kingdom) Brunel 13
(Richard Francis) Burton 14
Business Entrepreneurs 79

C
(Lewis) Carroll 13
Chessmen 64
Clone 74
Consulting Detectives 79
Covent Garden 37
Creating Paternoster Characters 79
Criminal 82
Criminal Gang 79
Cybershade 64

D
Dark Shadows 29
(Charles) Darwin 13
Debunking Myths 27
Defying Expectations 79
(Style of) Devices 85
Devices and Gadgets 85
(Charles) Dickens 12
Dividing the City 35
(The) Doctor and the Age 29
(The) Doctor's Victorian Adventures 29, 30
(The) Doctor's Victorian Companions 86
(Arthur Conan) Doyle 13
(Count) Dracula 28

E
Echoing the Golden Jubilee 21
(Father) Edward 66
Everything Changes and Nothing is as it Seems 18
Evoke the Era 18
Explorers 14

F
Factory Owner 81
Factory Worker 82
(Sir Douglas) Fairfax 54
(Nathan) Fairfield, 8th Earl of Redbury 54
Famous Personalities of the Age 11
Rosita Farisi 121
(Lord Alexander) Fitzstephen 48
(Gabrielle) Fitzstephen 48
(Jenny) Flint 118
(Rollo) Ford 68
Freckles 51
(The) Further Adventures of Jackson Lake 88

G
(New) Gadget – Artron Scanner 111
(New) Gadget – Holographic Emitter 60
Gentleman Adventurers 78
(Ada) Gillyflower 49
Grand Designs 10
Greater Lattitudes with Conceit 95
(Inspector Tobias) Gregson 50

H
Highgate Cemetery 45
(A Secret) History of the Late Victorian Age 20
History Through a Different Lens 16
(Madame Esther) Horowitz 51
How Capable 92

I
Inspiring Writers 26
(Be) Internally Consistent 20
Introduction 4
Investor 81
(The) Irish Question 21
It's a Team Effort 92

J
Jack the Ripper 22
(The) Jackson Lake Campaign 88
(Henry Gordon) Jago 122
(The) Jago and Litefoot Campaign 89
Jago and Litefoot Investigate 89
Josephine 75

K
(Dr) Karfelov 75
(Dr) Karfelov, the Borad and the Loch Ness Monster 73
Karratuddoranna 51
Korval 60

L
Labourer 81
(The) Labyrinth 38
(Jackson) Lake 120
Leper Hall 57
(A) Life in Service 82
Limehouse 39
(Joseph) Lister 14
(Professor) Litefoot 123
Literary Inspiration 97
(David) Livingstone 15
Loin Street 40
(Central) London 36
(East) London 38
(North) London 43
(South) London 42
(West) London 40
London Dock Strike 23
(The) London Stone 38
(Ada) Lovelace 14
(Miss) Lovelace 63
Lower Class Archetypes 81

M
(The) Many Faces of Clara Oswald 89
Marvels and Mysteries 10
(A) Matter of Class 8
(Lady Isobel) MacLeish 70
Me 58
(Gregor) Mendel 14
Middle Class Archetypes 81
(William) Morris 12
(The) Murder 39

N
(The) Napoleon of Crime 60
New Uses for Old Skills 98
(Florence) Nightingale 15
Noteworthy Places in Central London 37
Noteworthy Places in East London 39
Noteworthy Places in North London 44
Noteworthy Places in South London 43
Noteworthy Places in West London 41

O
(The) Occasional Flight of Fancy 94
(The) Old Bailey and Newgate Prison 37
(Clara Oswin) Oswald 124

P
(The) Palace Theatre 40
(Louis) Pasteur 14
(Creating) Paternoster Adventures 96
(The) Paternoster Campaign 92
(The) Paternoster Gang 87
Paternoster Investigations 87
Paternoster Irregulars 46, 78
Paternoster Row 37
(The) Paternoster's Guide to London 35
(Antoine) Petit 68
Philanthropist 80
Politician 81
(Adam) Poole 111
Poole's Ruffians 111
(William) Powell 12
(The) Prime Minister 53
(The) Principal Private Secretary 54
Professional 81
Progress in Leaps and Bounds 24
Publican/Barmaid 82

Q
Queen Victoria and the Royal Family 11

R
Raggedy Children 57
(The Revenant) Reverend 65
Reversing the Polarity of the Neutron Flow 96
(Allan Quincy) Riddell 71
Rogues' Gallery 55
Room to Breathe 19
Royal Observatory, Greenwich 43
Ryukyu Guardians 114

S
Scientific Investigators 78
Scientist 80
Scientists 13
(Mary) Seacole 15
(Alice) Shield 57
Shopkeeper 81
(The) Silver Nemesis 22
(Dame Regina) Smythe 52
Social Reformers 15
Spiritualism 25
(A) Steampunk Lens 97
(Mister) Steele 62
(Robert Louis) Stevenson 12
Strax 119
(A) Study in Flax 100
- 1. Queen Guinevere is Missing! 101
- 2. Pounding the Cobblestones 104
- 3. The House of Me 106
- 4. Heist Clean-up 108
- 5. Case Unexpectantly Closed 111
- 6. Temporal Workshop 112
- Adventure Synopsis 100
- Artron Echoes 110
- Beauty and the Beasts 110
- Betrayed 114
- Burleigh Street 102
- Clues at the Lyceum 102
- Cutting to the Chase? 104
- Edith Craig 103
- Ending the Adventure 115
- (The) Engine Room 113
- Interviewing Henry Irvine 102
- Judge, Jury and Executioner 107
- Luncheon Surprise 111
- (A) Matter of Memory 112
- (The) Mysterious Gentleman 104
- Napoleonic Gambit 109
- (The) Poole Gang 106
- Poole Party 110
- Possible Deduction 104
- Similar Disappearances 106
- (The) Stagehand and the Wasp 104
- Theatre is Politics 102
- (The) Zygma Experiments 100

(Sam) Swift 56

T
(The) TARDIS Cargo Delivery Company 44
(Types of) Technology 86
Technology Level 86
Temporally Tethered 93
(The) Ten Bells 40
(Sir Edward) Tolliver 70
(The) Torchwood Institute 69
Trader 82
(Bad) Traits 84
- Jingoist 84
- Know your Place 84
- Marginalised 84
- Persistent Illness 84
- Upper Class/Middle Class/ Lower Class 84

(Existing) Traits 85
(Good) Traits 83
- Agent of Scotland Yard 83
- Imprinted Memories 83
- Person of Repute 83
- Unthreatening 84

(New) Traits 83
Trap Street 38
TS-1953 114
(Frankiln) Tuttle 53

U
(The) Undercourt 44
Unnatural Magic 23
Upper Class Archetypes 80

V
(Scarlett) Valentin 66
(Madame) Vastra 117
(The) Victoria Waterfield Campaign 90
Victorian Adventurers 78
Victorian Adventures...in Space! 33
(The Late) Victorian Age 7
(The) Victorian Clara Campaign 89
(A) Victorian Conceit 94
(A) Victorian Out of Time 90

W
(Victoria) Waterfield 125
(Herbert George) Wells 13
What do we Mean by "Victiorian"? 8
When is Paternoster Investigations Set? 8
Who is the Dame? 52
Women and the Home 9
Writers 12

Y
Your Own Paternoster Gang 78